OUR SOUL'S JOURNEY

www.amplifypublishing.com

Our Soul's Journey: Empowering Wisdom to Live Your Best Life

Production, Art, and Design:

Producer & Project Direction by Talia To'omalatai-Thompson

Illustrations by Alosina To'omalatai-Thompson

Cover & Book Design by Safua Elisaia

For more information, please contact:

Amplify Publishing, an imprint of Amplify Publishing Group
620 Herndon Parkway, Suite 320
Herndon, VA 20170
info@amplifypublishing.com

Library of Congress Control Number: 2022909714

CPSIA Code: PRV0622A

ISBN-13: 978-1-63755-254-4

Printed in the United States

To my parents, grandparents, partner, siblings, and the rest of my family who have agreed to always show me unconditional love as we've played the game of life. Thank you for helping me to weather the storms through tears and triumphs. We have kept the legacy alive.

To my dearest friends and colleagues: you know who you are! The ones who are always there for me when the whole world is running out. Thank you.

To all my athletes I've coached and mentored during the last three decades who have blessed my life with lessons of determination, dedication, and teamwork.

To Taylor and all the 2020 loves I lost, thank you for showing me the true meaning of Grace.

A special thank you to Talia To'omalatai-Thompson who agreed to God's spiritual calling to walk beside me, listen to me, and use her talents to create Our Soul's Journey.

Dear Reader

If you or someone you know has ever experienced deep suffering, sadness, depression, or hopelessness, I believe you will find comfort in this book that has found you!

Within the pages of this book lay little tricks to understanding your own journey and how to not only feel your pain, but how to use it to grow stronger, braver, and better than before. Think of this as a written guide for your journey to a path toward empowerment.

The good news is your Source is with you always, and so am I. Our Source—regardless of how it's defined by you, perhaps as God, Universe, Energy, or Cosmos—is with you always.

If you don't believe in a higher power, I want you to pretend for just a second that miracles, angels, and life-changing synchronicities do exist and will show up for you while you complete *Our Soul's Journey*. Allow yourself to acknowledge the possibilities of life-changing experiences and miracles by documenting each gratitude that comes your way.

This book weaves coaching and encouragement to overcome struggle and win the championship called your *best life*. So let's go—come along and let us begin your path forward to amazing joy.

With love,

Our Soul's Journey

EMPOWERING WISDOM TO LIVE YOUR BEST LIFE

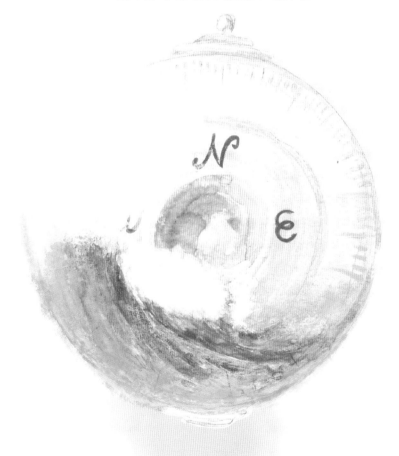

Kim Norman

amplify

an imprint of Amplify Publishing Group

Contents

Introduction

For Us

Before We Begin Our Journey

Chapters

Prologue

In this book, we will be taking a journey to empowerment, and my hope is that with every page you turn, you will imagine yourself in the scenic places that I have used to describe this path to empowerment. *Our Soul's Journey* is split into four parts:

Part One: For Our Bodies—Our Life's Garden

In this section, we will begin to understand the very first seedlings of who we are.

Part Two: For Our Hearts—Mountains, Peaks, and Valleys

In this section, we acknowledge our growth and learn to take risks that will create opportunities of great success.

Part Three: For Our Minds—Our Oceans

In this section, we explore the power of mindset and manifesting power. This section teaches us how to make our thoughts our things.

Part Four: For Our Souls—Our Lighthouse

In this section, we will arrive at the ultimate destination of blissful surrender in finding Source, self, and soul. We will discover our very own Savior ashore.

You will notice blank spaces throughout the book; these pages are for you. I invite you to write, paint, or draw out the emotions you feel with every question that is asked. It will help you to understand yourself better as you read my teaching memoir.

I pray that my experiences will send the universal vibrations needed to guide you through your life and lead you to a place of pure love for yourself and others. With every metaphorical step you and I take while writing and reading this book, may we all learn how to become the best versions of ourselves.

Here's to us and *Our Soul's Journey*.

"In the wind
the tree will bend,
in the wind
the branch will shake,
but in the end,
the deeply rooted
will be
too strong
to break."

—Morgan Harper Nichols

Our Source

As we embark on this *Empowerment Journey* together, we first get to help you define what your Source is. This vital step assures you are never alone. If you don't define it, you might never know where to draw your inner strength from during times of hopelessness and struggle—otherwise known as the *dark night of the soul*.

Many call their Source God, Universe, Energy, or Cosmos. These titles create an all-inclusive blend of religious and spiritual teachings from around the world. I have grown to appreciate the many faiths woven throughout the continents, because every faith has its own foundational story. Buddha was a prince who left his wealth and family. Moses led his people out of Egypt and through the Red Sea after being enslaved for centuries. Jesus Christ was an innocent man who was persecuted and crucified.

Though each faith paints a picture of great suffering, in the end, this suffering led to the light of love, peace, joy, and happiness. Although our Sources might have different names, your story and mine are no different: we are a generation that seeks the solution to deal with the suffering and the enlightenment to know we are on the path to peace!

My Source is God—the great I *am*. Who is your Source? My Source restores hope to my life. I believe that

within God, all things are possible.

I believe in the guidance from parables to mystical codes, the secrets of synchronicity and crystals that offer serenity to us all. My God promises that all darkness has a light at the end of the tunnel.

Source is an invisible essence and unlimited power that invites inner peace to change our lives.

I believe myself to be a part of everything that teaches us to love ourselves and love others. Because of my sexuality, I have dealt with countless religions that preach and teach that there is no place for me in Heaven. They preach that as a lover of

"Holiness comes wrapped
in the ordinary.

there are burning bushes
all around you.

every tree is full
of angels.

hidden beauty is waiting in
every crumb."

—Macrina Wiederkehr

people, of souls, of women, I can't have eternal happiness. The day I became a believer in Jesus Christ—the prince of peace who covered every shortcoming with His blood and sacrifice—the day I asked the Holy Spirit to dwell inside me, is the day I merged with the infinite source of abundance.

Knowing this power has allowed me the awesome gifts that are bestowed upon Earth through archangels, mystics, psychics, and powers the Universe has to offer. This is what I call my Source. My Source is love, kindness, forgiveness, family, and life's angels who walk beside me daily on this journey. Let's find your Source, that natural knowing that says, "I have you, every step along the way. You are not alone. I am with you always."

My prayer for you today is that you allow that Holy Spirit of life into your heart—allow it to grow, flow, and create your absolute best life—right here, right now!

How do we know if we have Source? For me, I believe in the teachings of Jesus Christ: "Ask and it will be given; seek and ye shall find." The key words in this principle are *ask* and *seek*. Notice how these are action-based words. To know if we have Source, we must first *ask* Source to dwell within us. The second point is to *seek* or *search* for answers that we may have.

The simplest way to find Source is to hear the words, "Be still and know I am God." Take time alone, and either out loud or silently go through the four Ws: who, where, when, and why. This lesson is used to seek (1) a solution to deal with the suffering, and (2) the enlightenment to know that we are on the path forward to our best life of joy and peace.

To assist you in finding your path, identify the four Ws of your Source.

Who

WHO IS YOUR SOURCE?

IS YOUR SOURCE GOD, ALLAH, BUDDHA, COSMOS, MOTHER EARTH, OR FATHER SKY?

As you look inside, ask yourself who your Source or spiritual guide is. Sit with yourself without distraction and still your mind. Once you're at peace and still, journal on who your Source is. A natural knowing will come over you; this is when you are at complete peace. It is when the soul and the Source become one.

You'll notice a physical feeling of peace and gratitude. Observe how you feel when you are in wonderment. It is that space where we sit in silence and reflect upon who we are. From wonderment comes the natural knowing of your true path.

Where

Our Source is all-knowing and everywhere, and we can feel Source within us always. After you've considered who your Source is, sit in gratitude for its presence. Feelings will come over you, both physical and emotional. Observe where these feelings are resonating. Do you feel warmth in your heart or head? Do you feel tingling in your feet or hands?

How is your heart? What kinds of emotions are being pulled to the surface? Do you feel relief? Joy? Light? Where do these feelings surface, your head or your heart? Journal about where you're feeling Source's presence. Note that as you continue on your journey, these sensations and emotions and their locations in your body and heart will change, and that's completely okay.

When

After you've considered the who and where of your Source, it's time to consider the when. As explained previously, Source is always with us and within us, but our relationship and acknowledgements of Source may change as we become more enlightened and connected.

Consider the place you're at now in your life. What challenges or fears are you confronting? Consider the time in your life you're in right now. Why do you think it is important for you to connect with Source right now, at this moment in life? Journal on the thoughts and feelings you encounter.

Why

WHAT IS YOUR WHY?

Deep down, everyone has a why, a reason for living and being. Your Source is connected, always, to your why, to your purpose. Consider what your core values are, the ones that drive you daily. These could be love, trust, loyalty, respect, or courage, among many others.

Our why is driven from what we want for ourselves, our families, our community, and the world. Changing the world is done daily by changing *your* world. Once *your* world changes, the rest of the world changes with it.

Once you identify your why, keep reminding yourself of it every day. In the hard moments, that reminder will pull you through.

When will you know you are enough? Life is short, and death is sure—don't wait another second—take one step today in the direction of your why. It doesn't have to be anything big; just do one thing. Hold a spiritual staff meeting and allow your requests and needs be known. This is a time when you sit intentionally and call on your spirit guides for connection and guidance. During your meeting, ask that they take the lead, and let them be the experts. Send them out confidently knowing they will return the with the answers you seek.

These don't even have to be the questions you ask yourself in a traditional way. However you decide to consider these questions, feel the answers and listen to the thoughts and emotions that will flow throughout your body, heart, mind, and soul as you encounter them. The answers will come in many forms; take notice as they synchronistically appear all around you. Focus on the answers that are given in the silence of those moments.

We must all learn to accept that none of us is perfect, and we all make mistakes. We are human beings. Source knows and loves us so much that whatever we think we lack, our Source will help us to understand and fully believe we are our own infinite sources of pure love, abundance, grace, hope, and peace. We are spirit beings having a human experience.

Whatever your Source may be, you must know and believe that the Source is infinite, perfect, whole, and complete. It has no lack nor limit. It is power, blessing, and grace. It is the first heartbeat. It is the first breath. It is you. You are one with your Source. You always have been, and you always will be.

The odds that any human would be *you* is 400 trillion to 1. Your arrival on the planet is a true blessing, thus showing that miracles do happen in your life.

How amazing is it that both your first heartbeat and first breath are a natural brilliance? You are *the* miracle. Know it, believe it, understand it. Ask yourself this question: Do you approach your life with the belief that you *can* and *will* continue to be a miracle creator?

For me, it's not always so simple.

It's never easy to stay afloat when you feel as though the waves and current are pulling you under. I've had moments of complete devastation, just as I'm sure you have. These were moments that made me question my worthiness of being a miracle creator.

The year 2020 was a hard one for me and an amazingly difficult time for our world. These difficulties have tested all of us. We have been taxed beyond belief, and we all have experienced loss, detours, and devastation. However, at some point, the weight of all the trials we face becomes heavy, and sometimes we need a second to just *be*.

After months of pain, betrayal, loss, and abandonment, the mass of it all came toppling down on me. The pressure of everything was so immense that I felt stuck. It was an overwhelming feeling of being stagnant and having no sense of direction. So, I participated in a full moon ceremony to release negative energy and attract my highest desires.

A Native American friend walked me through this ceremony where you write down everything you want to release for that month. Then you bless those things, thank them for coming, then put the paper in a fire and reflect on what you feel the fire is telling you. Then you write down everything that you want to attract and put that paper in the fire.

I asked to release anything from my life that was not serving the higher good. I wanted deep understanding and passion to release the stagnation and attract God's purpose for my life. As my written words began to burn, the flames fluttered out of the fire like a blue butterfly. A sure sign from God that something was coming, and that it was time for me to get back in alignment with my passion and purpose for life.

At that time, everything was in such disarray around me that I couldn't even talk anything out with my partner, who was also struggling with her own life and trials. She too felt a need to find herself again. The following night after the burning, the love of my life told me that she needed to leave because she felt that she was holding me back from my purpose. It was the catalyst of the final shotgun blow that spread every essence of my being to the stars. Thousands of pieces of me floated everywhere; my trying to pull it all together was the beginning of rediscovering the purpose of my life.

My partner leaving me so that we could find ourselves was an act of love. This was a reflection of the deepest commitment and understanding of one another. We knew we were not on the right path; she was the one strong enough to pull the trigger. The trigger I could have never pulled because I believe in infinite possibility.

To love them is to set them free so that you find you, and I find me; if it is meant to be—it will be. She needed to set me free. This book is a thank you to her for providing the catalyst for my life's introspection and creation of the path forward to my why.

After the breakup, I took a life time-out for myself, my mental health, and my overall well-being. I retreated for a few days to grieve the loss of the love of my life, but with the help of family and friends, I was able to create a healing space for my body, heart, mind, and soul. It was important for me to reconnect with who I was, what I needed to learn from this trial, and where I could go upon returning to reality.

To whoever is reading this, please know that whatever events happen in our lives—the good, the bad, and everything weaved in between—they are all blessings, though sometimes in disguise. We must go through the pain, tears, and triumphs to become who we were meant to be.

Our Soul's Journey has been the collection of over thirty years of written work, stories, and lessons, finally being braided together to create the message of understanding that when you think your life is falling apart, it is actually falling into place.

So, here I am, sharing my wisdom through my experiences, lessons, and recipes threaded throughout this book. Though I have already found my purpose, my hope is that you will find yours. Let us begin this journey together, you and I, with your Source and mine, hand in hand, as we walk through *Our Soul's Journey*, where sources, stories, and souls collide.

Who Are You? Who Do You Want to Become?

Your identity is essential to who you are and what you envision for your life. It's all about how you define yourself—your beliefs in their entirety.

> **Human beings will do anything to remain consistent with how we define ourselves, but our definitions of ourselves can change for the better . . . if we let them.**

When you discover who you are and begin living by it, your entire life will change. To make your vision happen, you need to become the type of person who can make your dreams a reality. It all begins with defining who that person is and who you want to be in this life.

Ask yourself these questions and write your answers on the given blank pages:

Who am I?

A lot of people in coaching want their players to call them "Coach," but I have a different perspective: I coach, but my name is not Coach. I am more than that. I am a human being, teacher, business owner, and leader. I am Kimberly Anne Norman. Who is she? She is not what she does. All these titles are a piece of the talents and gifts that I have, but I am not limited to what I do. Who I am is also the thoughts, feelings, and emotions inside my mind.

I am worry, stress, trials, judgements, and tribulations. I am joy, light, love, a child of the great creator God, an instrument of servitude.

It was often a joke with my athletes that I should write a Book of Norman; I never felt like I could after my college experience writing my thesis. It came back with blood red pen marks all over every page. This book is my attempt at being totally vulnerable and exposed and to offer hope with lessons that will guide my readers to their most amazing life. The experiences in this book are my life's journey. My hope

"'For I know the plans I have for you,' declares the Lord, 'plans to prosper you and not to harm you, plans to give you hope and a future.'"

—Jeremiah 29:11

is that they offer insight into how to create an amazing life of fun, happiness, trials, and epic failures. It is an attempt to do as God has called me to do: to offer creators love through my words, lessons, and experiences.

Teaching and coaching taught me who I was not. It got me asking these questions: *Who are you? What is your life's purpose?* Many are following the *do, have, be* or the *be, do, have* paths—it doesn't matter the order you put those words in, because if we do something to have something to be something, we are always going to be unhappy.

However, if me being me fulfills my purpose, I will have the greatest blessing of all: peace. I'm not doing something to have something to be something. I am being me to have something that is real. I'm aligned with my true self.

There will come a day when you are at the bottom, and you'll have to ask yourself: *Do I have a path to purpose, or do I even want to breathe today?* Because what is life without dreams? That life is dark, and it breaks my heart to know that some of the closest people to me are in that space of hopelessness. I know how cold it is, how scary, how paralyzing it is. I know how you absolutely need a guide. If you don't have an infinite Source, or God, ask sincerely for them to join you; they will help you during your soul's journey.

I pray this book will provide the comfort and teachings to bring you closer to your Source and give you a place to turn where you are never alone here on Earth. Reach out to us, we will guide you during your time of need, growth, or inspiration.

When we really know who we are, we can be who we say we are. I am a precious piece of my Source, joy, peace, and love. When our souls are still, who are we? Becoming our true selves is when we know peace inside regardless of the storms outside.

We all want to feel perfect, whole, and complete. But what does that feel like? What does that look like? All those heavy things we carry in our bodies, hearts, minds, and souls is what we are not.

It's okay if before beginning this journey, you believed you are what you do. The journey of this book is to let the readers know you are not only those things. You are all of that *and so much more*. What you do is what you were called to do or have to do. But who you are is peace, passion, and your true purpose. If you are currently struggling to know peace, passion, and purpose fear not. We are about to awaken within you the warrior that can do all things. Source is ready to shake it up. Regardless of where you find your power—from God, Source, Universe, Energy, Cosmos, or the Karma of Life—it will get you back on your path to peace.

Who are you?

Who do I want to become in this life?

When I began thinking about who I wanted to become in life, I remembered I wanted to be a nurse or a softball coach. I never really imagined being a doctor. It was a time when the expectation was that girls would be nurses and boys would be doctors, which is not as bad as the generation of my mother, but there were still barriers.

I was a part of the Title IX generation—the generation that, for the first time, mandated equal access to educational programs and systems that received federal funding, including sports programs. The boys practiced at the high school after school, while we had to walk a half mile to the middle school to practice. The boys had cheerleaders; we did not. We played the early game; the boys played the late one. Even when I started coaching in 1992, my teams were given the small gym, while boys got the big gym and prime time.

I was the team organizer for many of our youth volleyball teams. I would get companies to sponsor us, and then I'd load all my pals into my mom's Blazer and off we'd go, playing tournaments all over southern Utah.

As a young girl, I was attracted to the idea of running my own business. I used to go to the office with my dad and pretend that I was the boss. This was my earliest memory of becoming an entrepreneur. On top of that, I loved competition and sports. My high was anything that had a bat and ball, a net and a ball, or water and movement. I just absolutely fell in love with sports. They were my first true love.

Some years later, I was working on my degree in physical education at Utah State University (USU), and I ended up at a professional physical education convention in Boston, Massachusetts, as part of my training. It was there, while playing balloon volleyball at a dance at the convention, where I met John Kessell, who was the director of grassroots development at USA Volleyball. Since I was working with the USU women's volleyball program, he encouraged me to consider starting a Junior Olympic team out of Utah. Within weeks, I came home and started the Utah All Stars.

As time went on, I began training twenty-four young girls at USU one weekend a month. Convincing young athletes to play on Sunday in Utah was no easy feat because of how large a role religion played in their lives. From my college apartment, I incorporated Intermountain Volleyball Association (IVA) and started the first USA Volleyball Junior Olympic program. Three years later, I established another non-profit volleyball club called High Country Volleyball Club.

These programs grew from my college apartment to a 52,000-square-foot facility; that group of twenty-four Utah All Stars evolved into thousands of young women playing high-level USA Volleyball in Utah and Idaho. From 2002 to 2010, IVA hosted several USA Volleyball National Championships, posting a large economic impact to Utah. I also created a local program called High Performance so that top-level Intermountain athletes could compete worldwide. Later, USA Volleyball took the model and implemented the USA Volleyball High Performance program for all of its forty-nine regions.

I created High Performance because I believed that any athlete could become an Olympic athlete. I wanted to show that I could take twelve talented young women from Utah and Idaho, put them together on a team, and help them believe that—if given the opportunity—they could rise to greatness. From those efforts many great players—such as Brenda Barton, Logan Tom, Kristin Richards, Sydney Anderson, Airial Salvo, and Emillie Toone, to name a few—began to impact the USA Volleyball national system. We taught them to dream big and believe in the power of their dreams.

I remember telling Logan Tom at age twelve that she was going to be an Olympian. Four years later, she became the youngest player ever selected to play for an American Olympic volleyball team. Every dream starts with giving people the opportunity to try it, to believe it, and then be it. This is what I hope to teach the world through this book.

These accomplishments stemmed from my ultimate desire to help young women from the Intermountain Region play high-level volleyball. This created the opportunity to live out my passion of sports, business, and travel. The 1990s were an amazing time of growth for Utah and Idaho volleyball.

At this time, I was also a full-time physical education teacher. I taught at Highland High School, then Westminster College, and lastly at West High School. With each position, I would take the volleyball programs at these schools from failure to success.

It was the same story over and over. I would join programs that had never won, and we would build them up to multiple years of championships. We'd produce high-level collegiate recruits and earn awards. Eventually I would receive recognitions as coach of the year, and finally I became a member of the American Volleyball Coaches Association 400 Win Club.

Whether I am building volleyball teams, authoring a book, or building a destination resort, the goal is always the same: play hard, have fun, and dream big. I realize now more than ever that building a business, volleyball team, or family starts at the exact same place: a strong desire to serve, love, and guide people. I am eternally grateful that I get to connect and love so many different types of amazing people all while edifying God.

When you are being who you are, God will weave your dreams with your journey. That in itself is so scary. Do we want to sabotage our dreams, or do we want to believe in infinite possibility and dare to dream big, even if we might fail epically? I say dream your impossible dream, because you deserve to make it possible. Dreams are achieved with hard work, joy, and passion headed in the direction of your purpose here on Earth. Go create your dreams!

Now, how are you going to color your success? It's your power. Go do it. Answer the following questions, and use my sample answers for guidance.

Who do you want to become in this life?

If I were to look up my name in the dictionary, what would it say?

Kimberly, Kim, or Kimmy is an eccentric, frisky, and a hopeless romantic.

ec·cen·tric

ik'sentrik *adjective*

A person or their behavior that is unconventional and slightly strange.

frisk·y

'fri-skē *adjective*

Playful and full of energy.

hope·less ro·man·tic

'hōpləs rō'man-tik *noun*

A person who holds sentimental and idealistic views on love.

If you were to look yourself up in the dictionary, what would it say?

If there were no limits, who would I be?

If there were no limits, I would be the CEO of God's Heaven. I would be a creator. I would teach all over the world. I would have a beautiful place where people would come hang out, learn, retreat, grow, garden, feast, and laugh. It would be the world's ultimate playground. It would be fun and easy, and not exhausting, but enlightening. It would be a hike that's a stroll. A swim that's relaxing. A sun tan that's not too hot. It would be the tender blessings of life, and I would be the orchestrator of all of it.

If there were no limits, who would you be?

How would I define myself?

A passionate lover, friend, creator, and dreamer.

How would you define yourself?

What do I want in all dimensions of life?

Physical
To be healthy and robust like a twenty-one-year-old. To have a lot of stamina for all the amazing things in life. I want my smile to be contagious and to laugh a lot—the real deep belly kind of laughs. I want to be cute, but not too cute, with some fun hair and fun glasses. I don't want to be treated like I'm old or invalid. There's a saying that goes, "When we treat our parents like they're old, they get old," and I guess that just reflects my own thoughts and perceptions on people who are elderly. If we can balance respect and how we treat them by allowing them to feel youthful on the days they feel unseen, then we offer them a chance to continue living with purpose. Just some food for thought.

Emotional
This Buddha quote is one of my favorites to live by: "There is no path to happiness; happiness is the path." This is my emotional mantra—to live happily. For my own heart, knowing a peacefulness that cannot be rivaled. When I think of my heart and what would happen if I were to tap into it, I wonder what would be seen. I imagine an aura of white light and brilliant blues, with golden sparkles that flow from me like a soft waterfall. Feeling easy, glowing, and purely happy. As I've transitioned from a coach to a life mentor and guide, I realized that it's my destiny and my choice to only invite people in who seek and want that same flow of lighthearted happiness. You have the same choice too.

Psychological
I want to have the power to address the fears that lay within my mind. I want to be able to acknowledge their presence, but then give them permission to leave my mental space of living. I want to allow the infinite abundance of my God to work through all things without that limitation of fear or worry in my mind. I want to get to a place where I know that good is coming all the time, and that it is unconditional. I will trust that when I place a certain dream on my dream board, God will provide it or better, regardless of how it happens. His plan is perfect, and I get to eliminate that fear of not knowing what will happen next.

Social
A really cool network of souls that I play with, have fun with, and laugh with. A community that is easy come and easy go; one that is not needy, but healthy. A space with people who have similar values and objectives of peace and acceptance and those who seek true and vulnerable connection, love, and grace.

Spiritual

Lean on Source completely. To know, trust, and believe that the plan is perfect, on time, and fantastic. To balance the worldly desires within my body, heart, and mind that seep into my spiritual being. Stay grounded in my purpose of what my God intended me to do. To seek, guide, and love others. To teach the world of His works and allow my success to be a well of infinite abundance, light, peace, joy, and hope. To serve Him and be able to provide more than enough resources for the lost souls who so desperately need a friend in this world.

The summary of all of this—everything that I want in my physical, emotional, psychological, social, and spiritual dimensions of my life—is the glorious image of the tree from the movie *Avatar*. This film reminds all of us we must reconnect with our moral passion. It illustrates the need for us to teach a moral commitment to building bridges to human rights and environmental justice. I want this idea to be rooted in my beliefs and purpose.

To grow and connect with souls who seek to become who they were born to be. To know that as our roots deepen, as our branches stretch wide, and as we begin to let our flowers and fruits grow, we can flourish into our best lives. To understand what we truly value in our culture, and to never forget what values matter most to our lives. Work diligently to keep the poison out of our root systems so our tree of life will not die.

I imagine the world as a garden grove of these like-minded trees and people that stretch across the globe. Our roots begin to intertwine and weave together. Our fruits and flowers bud and blossom as we learn from our mistakes. Our energies synchronize to create these beautiful and magnificent bonds with human beings who seek connection, love, light, peace, and hope. Our souls blend with others who too are on this path we call life—this walk, stroll, and run through our *Empowerment Journey*.

What do you want in all dimensions of life?

Physical

_____
_____
_____
_____
_____
_____

Emotional

_____
_____
_____
_____
_____
_____
_____

Psychological

_____
_____
_____
_____
_____
_____
_____

Social

Spiritual

Exercise: Now that you've written out your ultimate vision, purpose, and identity, I invite you to bring this vision and dream of *who you are* and *who you want to become* to life. My first lesson for you is to design a dream board. This will give you the chance to create and manifest the dreams you have written into existence by matching your words with photos, quotes, drawings, and/or paintings that illustrate *who you are* and *who you want to become.*

This experiment of mine was an assignment for my 17s team from High Country Volleyball Club. I had the girls find ten images that represented who they were—both past and present—and ten images of who they wanted to become. The result: a room full of young women with a guiding light to a better and clearer vision of their bright and beautiful futures.

Now it's your turn to envision, create, and take the first steps to living and loving your absolute *best life.*

Lesson One
Our Dream Boards

Purpose: To identify who you are now. Take away all the limiting beliefs and become what you want to be. Drive your purpose to who you want to be. Dream your purpose forward.

Tools:

- A poster or corkboard
- Your written answers
- Visual materials like photos, paintings, words, and/or drawings

- Pen, pencil, or highlighter
- Scissors
- Glue, staples, thumbtacks, or tape

Activity: Create a dream board to reflect on throughout *Our Soul's Journey*.

step one:
Reread your answers that you have written for the following questions:
Who am I? Who do I want to become in this life? If I were to look up my name in the dictionary, what would it say? If there were no limits, who would I be? How would I define myself?

step two:
Circle or highlight words or phrases that stick out to you in your answers that explain who you are or who you would like to become. If you've written out words like *dreamer, lover, scientist, teacher,* or *artist, musician, lawyer, hair stylist, etc.,* mark these words.

step three:
Whether you have defined yourself or your future-self as an athlete, mother, dog owner, or friend, find visual materials that illustrate these words. If you're a volleyball player, draw or print a picture of a volleyball. If you're a mother, perhaps include a photo of your children. If you're a chef, snap a shot of your favorite dish to cook. Take your scissors and cut out all of your subjects. When you are done doing this, organize these images into two categories: *who you are* and *who you want to become.*

step four

After cutting, gathering, and organizing these visual materials, lay them all out on your poster or corkboard. On each half of the board, sort and place the images you have chosen for *who you are* and *who you want to become* in every aspect of your physical, emotional, mental, spiritual, and social being.

step five

Tape, glue, or staple these visual and/or written materials onto your poster or corkboard.

step six

Hang up or place your dream board in a space that you often spend time in. Whether it's your bedroom, your bathroom, or your garage, just put it somewhere that you know you will see it every day, multiple times a day. It will be your reminder of *who you are* and *who you want to become*. This will be your foundation as you begin your *Empowerment Journey*, because to know where you are going, you must first understand where you come from and the root of your identities.

Remember, this dream board is for *you*. It's so you never forget your vision. It's so you never forget your destination.

" The future belongs
to those who believe
in the beauty of
their dreams."

—Eleanor Roosevelt

Part One

For Our Bodies

Our Life's Garden

Everyone starts somewhere. Our greatest adventures
sprout from the seeds and roots of where
we come from. *Our Life's Garden* is the beginning
of our journey to truly know who we are.

Chapters

1

Our Seeds

My earliest childhood memories were playing in the dirt at my family property in Moab, Utah. Most days, I woke up; packed my bag with bottled waters, a peanut butter and jelly sandwich, and maybe a couple other snacks; threw it all on my horse's saddle; and off we'd go. The wilderness that surrounded my home was layered with the ancient history of fossils, arrowheads from the Native Americans who once hunted the grounds my father built our home on, and creatures that danced across the rich red soil. My fascination for life in its entirety—from the smallest ant to the tallest tree—was a base foundation of understanding that every person, creature, and plant has a beginning and an end. We all start as little seeds of life that take root in who we are, and we eventually grow or branch out to who we become.

Looking at our lives as a garden has great symbolism to how we approach *Our Soul's Journey*. From the moment the sperm meets the egg, we have DNA planted as the form of an embryo. We carry the magic of that first seed with us from beginning to end.

In the *Mindbody Code* by Dr. Mario Martinez, he states that "25 to 35 percent of who we are is in our DNA." The rest, however, are the seeds of thoughts and emotions that form our personalities—who we *think* we are.

We begin the planting of thought with beautiful seeds of perfection and color. Seeds that reflect an attitude of *I can do anything*.

We plant seeds of behavior, and from those seeds come the beauty of action and reaction.

As we begin the growing cycle, these emotions and behaviors take root and begin to flourish in our gardens. Here's the catch: If any of these emotions or behaviors have thorns of doubt, lack, or limit, they also take root. If we planted positive attitudes and behaviors, they too will flourish. This is when mindsets get fixed and

"Life does not
accommodate you,
it shatters you.

It is meant to,
and it couldn't
do it better.

Every seed destroys
its container
or else there
would be no fruition."

—Scott Maxwell

established; these are the roughly 60,000 thoughts we think about daily and water. The flowers of attitude, behavior, actions, and results begin our spiritual gardens, planting the belief and the outcome of our amazing garden. This book will give us the skills needed to become expert gardeners of our life's garden.

> **"Life does not accommodate you, it shatters you. It is meant to, and it couldn't do it better. Every seed destroys its container or else there would be no fruition."**
>
> —Scott Maxwell

Think of your body, more specifically, your DNA, as the first *seeds* of your garden. You had no control of the seeds that were planted to create you. And most of the time, you have no control of the seeds planted that shape you into who you are. What I'm talking about are the experiences or events, both good and bad, that happen to us. These are the seeds that we often either really love or really hate. Most of the time, there is no in between. When we are born, we are born with a garden that is gorgeous and fertile, and as we go along in life, the wind blows in weeds that spread and plant around the parts and pieces of us that are beautiful.

I was born into an amazing and blessed life with privilege, love, and opportunity. I had parents who loved me, grandparents who adored me, and two younger brothers whom I spent time teasing, playing, and competing with my whole life. Though there were many moments of bliss, happiness, and light, the reality is that there were also times so dark that I didn't know if I ever wanted to share it. It takes bravery to unveil your past. So, here is my first attempt to be brave for you and for me.

As a child, I experienced what many of my readers will relate to—the unwanted and undeserved violation of sexual abuse. These traumatic experiences occurred before the age of ten at the hands of so-called family friends. Little did my parents know, these men were not friends. They forced the first unlovable seeds into my beautiful and innocent garden. For a long time, I never knew how to deal with the awful memories that haunted my physical being. My body was a gift from God, and here I was, hating it for what happened to me. No matter how hard I tried to destroy these seeds that began to grow in my garden, they spread like a weed and poisoned my blossoming flowers, plants, and trees. These seeds were thorns that got thrown into my garden, and they took hold and crafted a large part of me, giving me a growth that my family and friends could never understand.

Through this deep vulnerability comes my personal experiences of exposure that is real, authentic, and scary, and it's opening up a whole new perspective. Now, I realize that I cannot discard these unlovable weeds in my garden. It is a significant part of my story and my relentless will to survive. It is a part of that other 65 to 75 percent that can be replanted over and over again, until I turn it into something more than a poisonous weed.

We are all born infinitely whole, complete, and perfect. Our gardens are gorgeous and beautiful . . . but shit happens. Weeds blow in, and things get planted there that should have never been planted. It's not my parents' fault, or anyone's fault; stuff happens, that is called life. However it gets there, we must all try to understand that most human beings want what is best for us—and Source does as well.

Source isn't doing any of this to us. Source is allowing man to be man, and Source to be Source. Life teaches us what the gardener knows. The more fertile the soil, the easier it is to plant, but arid terrain will also produce gardens; it just creates a harder time for the seeds to sprout. I am thankful for my life, as it has made me strong and so appreciative for all of life's garden boxes I've learned to grow through.

Our life's garden is the foundation of who we are, but *Our Soul's Journey* is the path we walk back to enlightenment. It is understanding that each plant, flower, tree, or weed has its place in our garden. If our garden becomes overgrown, we get to use our amazing creative power to make the next season's flower bed better than the one before. All these plants are a part of you and a part of the amazing body of your life. To dig them up, bury them, or try and destroy them means you harm the roots of yourself.

New seeds will be planted throughout our life. Some will provide vibrant color for a season, as the annuals do, and some, like the perennials, will come back year after year, giving us the assurance that many parts of our garden will always bloom in their season beautifully, if they are tended to with all the right fertilizers and care from our hands, thoughts, and dreams.

Life is our garden. There is a season for all things under Heaven. Like Ecclesiastes 3:1-8 says.

"To every thing there is a season,
and a time to every purpose under the heaven:
A time to be born, a time to die;
a time to plant, and a time to pluck up that which is planted;
A time to kill, and a time to heal;
a time to break down, and a time to build up;
A time to weep, and a time to laugh;
a time to mourn, and a time to dance;
A time to cast away stones, and a time to gather stones together;
a time to embrace, and a time to refrain from embracing;
A time to get, and a time to lose;
a time to keep, and a time to cast away;
A time to rend, and a time to sew;
a time to keep silence, and a time to speak;
A time to love, and a time to hate;
A time of war, and a time of peace."

—Ecclesiastes 3:1-8

We must not be afraid of the unlovable seeds that are planted in our garden. We must also not be afraid to step away and experience life as it comes. Our roots will always be with us; they will follow and thread as we walk along the journey to empowerment. Compare each seed, plant, flower, or tree to people, memories, and experiences in your life.

We can always look back over our life and say *woulda*, *shoulda*, or *coulda*, but then we would have *shoulda* all over us. This book is intended for the reader who is ready to look at their life, celebrate its vibrant colors, and explore the tools and practices laid out in this book. The hope I have for my readers is that you will take this time to understand yourself better. If you're reading this and so happen to be near your dream board, take a second and look over it. Notice that a lot of the board is covered with images that help you define yourself and how you visualize the root of your personality or essence. Now, think back to defining moments that you think had an influence on who you are today.

Are these moments weeds or flowers? If they're weeds, dig them out. Break them, and learn from them; you do not have to let them overgrow and take over your life. If these moments are flowers, continue to water them, care for them, and let these beautiful plants dot along your path. Carry these with you as you live and learn more about yourself.

Life requires the blend of blessing and tragedy. It is both a rose and thorn. With the healing of time and forgiveness of ourselves, and perhaps others who have planted unlovable seeds in our life's garden, we will be able to gain strength.

Plant the garden of your dreams. Setting the weeds of pain into their own planter will help you to grow a beautiful planter of all your dreams. There is blessing in the reaping. Remember, *you reap what you sow.*

Lesson Two

Plant Something and Watch It Grow

Purpose: Life is our garden. We must grow through what we go through. Now it's your turn to evaluate your garden. Consider these questions:

- What values and cultural beliefs have been passed on to you that make your life work?
- Which values and beliefs limit and hold back your life's goals and dreams?

Looking at our lives as a garden has great symbolism to how we approach *Our Soul's Journey*. Write down your top three values and top three cultural traits. Plant only the seeds you want to grow.

Activity: We are going to plant a herb garden for our windowsills. With every seed you plant, visualize replanting your life's garden toward your purpose, and think of the values you've just identified. Commit to daily journaling about how the germination of that seed must feel, growing into its most vibrant self, and picture the same growth occurring within your soul.

Tools:
- Planter/pot
- Potting soil
- Plant seeds
- Garden markers

step one:
Using discarded teapots, suitcases, and drawers is a fun way to repurpose materials for a planter or pot and create fun and beauty around your home. Make sure to drill holes in the bottom of your repurposed materials for adequate drainage.

step two:
Go outside and find little pebbles around your yard, the street, or a park. Put a thin layer of these collected pebbles and rocks at the bottom of your planter or pot. Fill your pot or planter with soil to about three-quarters full.

step three:

Poke holes in the soil and sprinkle in your seeds. Cover the seeds with the excess soil. Wet this mix with warm water, and make sure to keep it moist.

step four:

Place your planter or pot near a window where it can receive sunlight. Water daily and speak kind words to your herb garden. Watch it grow, and journal every so often the growth you witness. Compare this new growth to your seeds, both lovable and unlovable, in your own life's garden.

(2)

Our Masks

While I'm writing this, it's 2020—the year the COVID-19 pandemic began. Our world is in mass hysteria; people don't know who to trust, who to vote for, or whether or not masks are a violation of our rights or a way to slow down the virus. I'm a rebel, so ultimately, I find myself on the fragile line of being told what to do but not following the rules as consistently as required.

It's such a strange time to be alive. Everywhere I see people with masks and without masks, and sometimes I wonder who is right. Is it the ones who follow the rules, or the ones who sense something is odd and risk the chance of becoming a host of the virus? There are so many things not adding up. In strenuous times like these, I am grateful to know the values I stand for and the beliefs that bring me peace. You must know what you stand for. It is important to figure out what seeds made you who you are today, and why you think, react, or act the way you do. Because it is in times where a mask is required to enter a majority of places, that you cover up yourself for the world to see.

Our identity is our most recognizable feature of who we are. The color of our skin, our eyes, our hair, our freckles, wrinkles that show our age, lips to plump our face, the list goes on. Masks however, cover these facial features up, and they often give the illusion that we are able to hide who we really are. But, if you really think about it, weren't we all technically wearing masks every day before they were required? Of course, I am not talking about tangible ones, but rather the masks we pull up to veil who we truly are.

Our metaphorical masks, as beautiful as we can make them, hide the remnants of suffering, disconnection, betrayal, shame, and pain.

Let's explore the masks we wear, what they are, why we wear them, and what beautiful pieces of our true selves they hide.

"Be yourself.
Everyone else
is taken."

—Oscar Wilde

Putting on a mask is a transformative experience that has been shared across cultures for centuries. Brazilian carnivals dating back to the seventeenth century, Mexico's Day of the Dead, the Carnival of Venice, and even Halloween are all cultural celebrations that use disguises that have been passed down throughout world history. The masks used for these celebrations allow us to be someone or something we are not, for at least a moment, changing both how we see ourselves and how we behave outwardly to the world around us.

Everyone wears a mask, not a physical one necessarily, but an alternate persona of some sort. We bury the parts of us that we are afraid to show, share, and connect with. Brené Brown has written that people are seeking connection and belonging, but masks are the way of keeping us separated, disconnected, and alone. Our facades lead to self-destructive behaviors, and most of the time we are oblivious to the effects these masks have on us. We hide behind our facial expressions, makeup, headphones, cell phones, social media posts, clothing, food, drugs, alcohol, and all other combinations of disguises that bury the true problems we are afraid to show. Our masks come from issues around *self-love*. We pretend things are great at work, at home, and in the classroom to keep up the image that *we are fine*. The harsh truth is there are times in life we are *not* fine. This book is to help us all acknowledge this and address the lies we bury to hide our honest selves from others. The true bravery is showing others that we have masks and that we also have the strength to work deep at our core to bring the walls down and create the connected life we all want, desire, and need.

What would happen if the ones you love the most knew who you *really* were? What we find out is that this is where real relationships, bonds, and connections collide. Being *you* is the best and most perfect thing you could ever do for yourself. As Oscar Wilde said, "Be yourself. Everyone else is taken."

Learning to love myself has always been a battle. I struggle with insecurity around picture-taking, worried that my hair, clothing, or smile are not good or pretty enough. This brings the mask question into play: What would I feel if I got to wear a costume for the photo shoot? Would I be as hesitant? Would the mask, revealing only eyes that sparkle and shine, be easier? It's all the same concept. Why is it that I would be okay to pose in front of a camera with something covering everything except my eyes? Vulnerability does not allow me or you to remain hidden. How can we all learn to consistently strip off the masks we wear to reveal our true selves?

Because I was sexually abused at a young age, I did not have the ability to communicate my feelings or understanding of the situation. This weed was buried deep in my subconscious mind, where most children place pain. My unconscious strategy of survival was to put on the mask of tough, competitive hard ass. Feeling shame, guilt, and betrayal led me to pretend that everything was fine, even though I had sabotaging relationship behaviors. A hug from my father was often uncomfortable and scary. I could never share with him why, and that it was not him. I loved my father immensely, but I struggled with the physical power and strength he had as a man. I did not realize many of my behaviors until I did the work to clear the fear of weeds planted in my childhood garden.

I wasn't able to create a life of honesty until I faced the identity behind this mask. The real identity behind this facade was hurt and broken and needed love and light. Not to be shunned and hidden behind my disguise.

These masks are so powerful. They have protected us, and they have been there when we couldn't or didn't know how to care for ourselves. They have been our barriers we put in place to keep the world from seeing who we truly are.

I am gay. This has been God's way of giving me the tender love of another without fear. Knowing that my family values did not line up with this choice has not been easy. Hiding behind the shame of being gay destroyed several partnerships with amazing women because we hid from the acknowledgement of our love. I wanted a family, and in each relationship, I got one. I wanted to marry my life partner and not feel the shame of society. Each time, without even realizing it, I would sabotage my own life and ruin what was built, just to start over. The pain of abandonment, betrayal, and shame would not allow me to feel, love, joy, and peace.

The first people I was ever honest with about my sexuality said to me, "We knew. We don't know why you waited so long to share the real you with us." So, thank you, Eric and Valerie for loving me *so* much!

Because of these genuine human beings in my life and the many more who have accepted and loved me for being me, I have been able to match the reflection in the mirror with the face looking back.

There are many reasons why we should shed our masks.

The first reason is to *strive to live a genuine life of fire*. A life filled with passion and happiness to reach our true potential. Being the real you with everything you do will allow you to feel the joy for the life you deserve. As you know, there is only one you! Others can do many of the things you can do, but what my God and your Source have called us to do are our own personal paths.

"It is so wonderful when you meet someone who already has their mask off in this masquerade of life."

—P.T. Berkey

Take a second to think about how many masks in a day you wear. What are some of the masks you wear? Describe them below.

I feel terribly unworthy some days talking to others about living their best life when I too struggle. I know Source would want every person I meet to know that my life experience has a wonderful message of hope. What I am teaching can and will assist you in finding your way to peace and happiness. There is a way to love the parts of us that have been abandoned, hurt, and harmed. We have to pick up those broken pieces of ourselves, place them in their proper place in our garden, and walk along our path, while lovingly reminding ourselves that we can do hard things and that life is full of wonderful summits. There are times we have to ask parts of our garden to wait a minute, trust us, and be patient while we figure out what we want. This is where training as a professional life coach will guide you through the soul's journey lessons into the light that allows you to rest, live, and laugh out loud.

The second reason we should shed our masks is *peace*. It is exhausting to live an inauthentic life, and it takes so much energy to hide the real you.

Take a second to think about how many masks in a day you wear. What are some of the masks you wear? Write or draw your feelings; you can use the space on the opposite page. Painting your feelings is a really fun way of letting pain bodies release from our subconscious.

I had a young athlete who spent significant amounts of time every night choosing her outfit for school the next day. She's a beautiful girl, both inside and out, and yet one of the *most* important things to her is her clothes. The way she looks to others is very important to her. She told the team that what her friends say to her each morning as she arrives at school decides whether it will be a good day.

This quote is a favorite: "Your opinion of me is none of my business; my opinion of me is all that matters." Puberty is a difficult time; it is when the world begins to tell us our role in society. Peer pressure is real, and it hits us everywhere. But I often wonder: *Why does this have to be the stigma we set ourselves up to believe? That what we wear and how we look to others is the* most *important thing?* It's one of those masks that we pull out each morning and paint on. What a heavy and exhausting mask to wear.

Now, I'm not saying that self-care and self-love should be looked down on, but rather let us take a step back and really evaluate these words. *Self-care* and *self-love*. The key word is *self*. The way we perceive ourselves, our true and natural selves, should be more important than how others view us. If we spend a while picking out the perfect outfit the night before school, or put on makeup to cover up a few blemishes, freckles, or wrinkles, let us do it for ourselves and not for others. This is for our own *peace*.

The third reason we should shed our masks is the *true love, you love*. How many of your masks are keeping you in self-talk that is negative and destructive? What part of these masks are keeping you in self-judgement? The realization that my thoughts were separating me from the very people who loved and cared about me was not understood until very late in life...way too late actually. I want to encourage you to speak up about thoughts and feelings that are separating you from self-love. How might you be sabotaging your true love? Why would withholding parts of ourselves be unworthy of love?

In our relationships, we can't be truly healed unless we offer up all the pieces. It's like handing someone a puzzle, but hiding the last few pieces. Masks allow us to sit on the sidelines, wondering why we are always practicing but never get to play. Stop cheating yourself. Allow yourself to play the messy game of life. Love yourself with reckless abandon. Others will love you and treat you as you treat yourself. When we have self-love, we have less tolerance in our lives for those who will cheat and remain hidden behind their masks of abandonment, fear, and shame.

We are all born perfect, whole, and complete. You can do this work; take off the masks if you really want to.

Lesson Three
Get to Know Your Masks

We've got to take off all the masks and layers to become our true selves of peace, love, and joy. As the poet e e cummings wrote, "The greatest battle we face as human beings is the battle to protect our true selves from the self the world wants us to become."

Purpose: I want to explore the masks we wear, what they are, why we wear them, and what pieces of our true self they hide. Masks—as beautiful as we make them—hide the remnants of suffering, disconnection, and pain. Before beginning the activity, complete the following prompts in a notebook:

Write about a genuine life filled with passion and fire. What does it feel like to deserve this life? Write "I am" statements in your response. *I am happy, I am peaceful, I am rich,* etc.

Experience peace. Write or list what things in your life are creating exhaustion and separation from your most authentic self? It is exhausting to live an inauthentic life, and it takes so much energy to hide the real you.

Stop cheating yourself. Allow yourself to play the messy game of life. What can you change today to get closer to your dream life?

How many of your masks are keeping you in self-talk that is negative and angry?

Which is separating you from the very people whom want to love you, the people who care for you and want to be in a relationship with you? How are you sabotaging your true love? Are there parts of yourself that you are hiding? If so, why?

Love yourself with reckless abandon, then you cannot be cheated. Others will love you and treat you as you treat yourself.

Activity: Paint a mask.

Tools

- Paper

- Paints

- Paint brushes

step one:

Grab a canvas or a piece of paper, and draw your mask. Add each of the different colors that describe your emotion on the mask you are drawing or painting.

- Red: Anger, embarrassment, passion, or lust
- Blue: Shyness, sadness, or calmness
- Yellow: Cowardice, happiness, or caution
- Green: Disgust, envy, friendliness, or greed
- Purple: Pride, fear, or courageousness
- Grey: Depression, regular sadness, or stoicism
- Black: Coldness or mournfulness

step two:

After you have completed your mask, take a look at what you see looking back at you. Take out your journal and write about your mask; tell its story. Once the story is written, anything you do not like can be rewritten. You get to then repaint the mask to reflect the feelings and emotions you want to put on each day as your daily reminder. Have fun creating your new facial attitude.

Our Judgments

judg·ment

/ˈjəjmənt/ *noun*

the ability to make considered decisions or come to sensible conclusions.

Most of our judgements are about learned bias, past experiences, happiness, or pain. Our brains are wired to make automatic judgments about ourselves, others, and situations. It is part of the fight-or-flight survival behaviors that allow us to move through the world without spending too much time or energy on understanding everything we see. Sometimes we engage in more thoughtful, slow processing of others' behaviors. But most of the time, our judgements are trained behaviors based on years of experience and practice. Any thought that I am having that makes me feel frustrated, anxious, not enough, sad, or disconnected can be summed up as a negative judgement.

How do we work on the discernment of knowing what judgements are disconnecting us from Source, self, and soul? We choose to judge others due to who we are behind the masks we wear. We judge from our own issues with betrayal, shame, abandonment, and fear.

Our judgments hold our fears and separation in place. We are created for connection. I'm not saying that caution should not be considered at times. For example, is the homeless person you encounter on the street just poor and destitute, or is the stranger running toward you a threat to your personal safety? We do need to judge our surroundings for safety, but angels are sent in all kinds of disguises to test us and see if we can extend an act of kindness and compassion. The test of true human connection is if we can offer an essence of love in a world of harsh judgement based on appearance.

The COVID-19 pandemic is a perfect example that we are currently facing as I write this chapter. Intense judgement and fear exist around the world. Fear of contracting the deadly virus and not surviving it or taking it home to someone we love. There

What judgments of others do you need to release?

are so many varying directives from authority figures and evaluating and judging the mandates is critical to our survival. We are expected to stay at home and stay six feet away from others. We are told to wear masks, and also to not wear masks. We are told the virus spreads by talking. It might spread by touching your face; but then how do we safely wear a mask? The expectation of us to comply with so many conflicting orders creates a constant need for judgement. Finding the sources to fact-check against is wrapped in propaganda and fear. The brightest doctors and scientists cannot agree on any one given path or method to solve this critical problem. This leaves the entire world operating upon its own judgement, knowledge, and best guesses of natural knowing.

Worldwide, our species is judging everything. Some are freezing and unable to move; others are fighting and not supporting the mandates. Others are in between, gauging what works best for them, their families, and the world. According to the Proceedings of the National Academy of Sciences, the fear was real for 43 percent of Americans who had no income while their businesses were shut down without choice or conversation. This has created real fear: not knowing how to pay bills or feed your family has magnified judgement for simple survival.

With everything going on, how do we feel in control and effective with information and change? These questions are answered when we go inside to Source and be still and look for all the positives you can find in the difficult situations. We can control how we live today. We get up, make our bed, create the task list to complete, and connect in innovative ways with people whom we care about.

During the pandemic, I felt trapped and lonely with my household emptying just a month before. Tears were shed for a long time, but I started creating ways to connect with new souls who were also searching for a safe space to talk and connect. Amazingly, I met some really great humans who chose connection over fear. I am thankful every day that God filled every one of my needs perfectly.

On the other side of the story, I had to be patient with other significant people in my life who needed to be socially distant and isolated; they needed the time and space to figure out how to address their fears and beliefs around the data and information. Complete empathy was required for all the souls on this journey trying to figure out which way of life worked best for them.

Wayne Dyer taught:

> **"There is your way; there is my way.**
> **They both are *the way!*"**

When we allow for individual differences and observe the decisions people make neither as right nor wrong, but rather as *their way*, it settles down the need to change someone.

It is extremely difficult to not judge, and what I have learned through study is that judgment is a part of our human existence. In *A Course in Miracles* it is written, "the ego cannot survive without judgement." As we take a closer look into what and where we seek our information, we get an immediate saturation of ego, thus boosting and judging information presented to us. The moment we swipe our cell phone, the dopamine begins to follow, and we begin placing images into our mind. We judge each and every image against the image of ourselves. With each swipe, we ask these things over and over again: *Am I enough? Am I pretty like them? Am I skinny like them?* We judge our personal worthiness, and we make instant decisions on someone else's worth and value to our lives.

Our social media accounts or other options record who we are or who we want others to think we are. It is perhaps the most dangerous mask of all. The fear we have of showing vulnerability through these accounts is self judgement and doubt. We do not see people sharing their life struggles. All the accounts are snippets of the peaks in life or the extreme valley of death. More people are turning to drama media—the place to expose judgement, hate, fear, and disconnection.

Why should we care how the world sees us?

We are not our looks. I've been there. I've been the self-critic who cannot find peace. Unable to live in my own skin due to self-judgement about my sexuality, weight, and appearance. Trying to figure out what we are protecting beyond our layers is not easy, right? As we look at the judgements, where do they start? When do we begin to evaluate our looks? When do we make the decision that we are beautiful or not beautiful? And who decides? Who decides that we are beautiful? It is every-body *but* us. It's scary to go inside and ask: *Who am I? What am I? What do I want?*

Throughout my life, I've struggled with my weight. I've asked the same questions many times to help figure shit out. How often are we taken off our life's course because someone else is deciding for us? And we let them. People only treat us badly because we let them, but we have the power to change this. Natural knowing allows us to be protected. We can be who we are—genuinely and authentically—once we decide to live in our own skill. Period.

The greatest judgements of my life are being bossy, driven, female, and gay. Powerful women are bitches. Powerful men are CEOs. I have lived with great shame

"My wish, indeed my continuing passion,
would be not to point the finger in
judgment

but to part a curtain, that invisible
shadow that falls between people,
the veil of indifference to

each other's presence,

each other's wonder,

each other's human plight."

—Eudora Welty

for being gay. I could not love myself because of the disappointment I felt that I caused. I thought I disappointed God, my parents, and my friends. I kept the secret and denied my feelings for a very long time. It was a dark place of abandonment and shame. My hope is that my message of release and removal of self-judgement allows you, the reader, to let go of all that negative self-talk. Set yourself free to *be*! Just as Robin Roberts says, "Make your messes your message."

 I think when we can create conversations and opportunities that allow us to be in a space where we can share our stories, we instantly become connected to the person we are behind the masks as well as the people we are constantly interacting with.

The collective experiences we all have allow us to relate to one another, and this is powerful beyond reason. To know and understand that every person has a story, is to know that we are all a part of a higher purpose and connection with each other. In life, we experience these pockets of great joy, but we also experience these moments of hell on Earth. Speaking out loud, I find myself fighting moments of disconnection and despair. What I have come to learn is that sometimes it is okay to be at peace with the battles we face. That sometimes, we need to just sit and feel, rather than get up and move around to try and ignore or to try and hide from the ickiness we feel inside.

Many individuals use the unlovable seeds planted in their life as elements that weight them down. They use these excuses of, "This happened to me in the past, so this is why I am the way I am today as an adult." We definitely have to learn how to work through those messy parts of our garden, or we will continue to carry it throughout our lives.

The journey to your life's harvest starts with asking for help during the struggle.

Connection begins with honest vulnerability. Deciding to remove the barriers and your protective masks allow fear of judgement to lose its grip.

When we can truly offer empathy, love, and forgiveness to ourselves, then we call out to the Universe a vibration that creates a powerful Law of Attraction for new vibrational energy that we choose to put in place of the old judgements, disconnections, and fears.

Loving every part of you unconditionally requires taking off the mask of judgement and allowing the essence of your purest soul to emerge authentically.

Lesson Four
Pain Purge

Purpose: Deep relationship connections are when we feel seen, heard, and valued by the ones we love. Take a moment to reflect on your relationships and the depth of your connections. How would you rate your relationships on a scale from 1 (always ending in abandonment and pain) to 5 (amazing, loving, and deeply bonded at home, work, and play)?

Let go of your past so that the past does not dictate the future. To eliminate the constant loop of events that tend to repeat themselves as we create life from day to day, implement the Pain Purge to exhaust emotions that are stored deep inside. Allow yourself to feel the emotions. Be willing to accept the feelings and the emotions. Numbing emotions with drinking, drugs, and anger just masks the pain. Stop hurting yourself and others.

Tools:
-Journal

Activity: Finally feel and release the pain you've kept inside yourself.

step one:
Find a safe place, allow your body and mind to expel all the hidden pain bodies stored up inside. Feel the emotions deeply and explode. If you need to scream at the top of your lungs or feel angry and punch a pillow, do it—get really mad. Do not hold even one emotion inside. Feelings and emotions are stored energy. The Pain Purge is you allowing your body, mind, and spirit to honestly express sadness, hate, anger, or jealousy, and let it all go.

step two:
Choose self-healing with acceptance and self-love. Once you have purged the pain, you need to make a decision. Accept the situation and choose yourself. By choosing yourself, you choose to move on, take control, end the victim dialog, and step into your personal power of choice.

step three:

Forgive everyone involved. Forgiveness is strength; it is important to remember that forgiveness is not forgetting what happened, it is the freedom from what happened. It allows you to have your power over it back. It requires great strength, for only the powerful can forgive. It is easy to stay angry and hurt forever, but the strong who can endure the pain achieve their greatness. Forgive the situation that brought the raging sea crashing on your shore. Forgive the person who hurt you, and most importantly, forgive yourself.

step four:

Write what you have discovered about yourself during the Pain Purge. What has this lesson taught you about your life's perseverance, patience, pain, and suffering? How has this pain made you stronger and more deserving of your best life?

(4)

Our Disconnections

We humans go to great lengths to numb our disconnections and judgements. The reason drugs, sex, alcohol, food, pornography, and money can be so powerful in our disconnections are that the numbness allows us to move to a space that says: "I don't want to feel *me*." The important question in these moments is: *Who is me*? Who is the person we are struggling so hard to keep behind these masks, to avoid being judged? If we can learn how to work through our gardens, water and weed, and understand every part of us, then we will not seek relationships with others who do not have our best interests in mind.

Growing up, I was afraid of revealing my true self, like many of us who have endured betrayal, pain, and suffering. At the age of fifteen, I was caught with my first girlfriend. Imagine the shame that was experienced. It was during a time when people who were gay were cast out from society. My family inevitably wanted that part of me to remain hidden. The shame I felt about myself created so many feelings and emotions to be buried deeply in the shadows of my life's garden.

My college years were some of the most difficult for me emotionally. I turned to substances that allowed me a way to ignore and numb my thoughts and feelings of not being enough. My friends and I would gather for parties that most of the time ended up being wild nights of complete disconnection from our bodies and minds. There were times when a person could be doing the most chaotic thing, or experiencing a high that was uncontrollable, and all the while, here we were, bodies wasted and minds splattered, laughing our asses off.

The only thing that kept me from becoming an addict was the fact that those of us who were student athletes had to find some sort of balance. Even though we could party hard on Friday nights just like the other kids, we also knew that Saturday morning conditioning was just as real as the substances we were using. I thought these disconnectors were the way to happiness. In truth, these substances were just

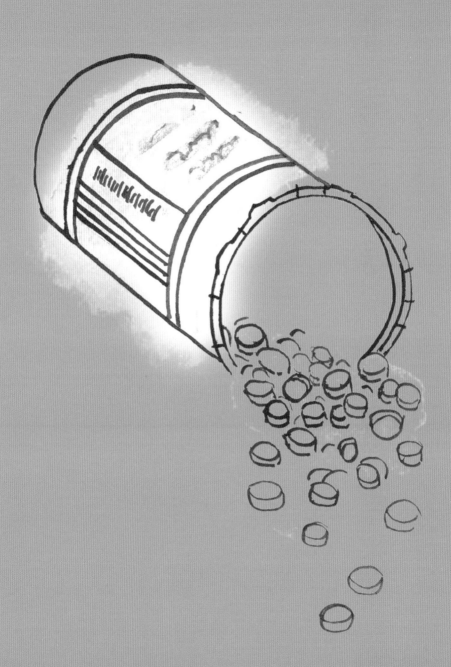

delaying me from dealing with the pain that would wait until explored, embraced, and guided into their appropriate beds within my life's amazing garden. There's not much that a kid could do today that would shock me. Until this day, I don't know where I would be without sports.

On top of the painstaking substance abuse I put myself through, food was another disconnector used to create my mask of weight. It was the solace of an over-portioned meal that allowed me to bury my feelings alive. I did not realize I was using food as a way to separate my true self from the person I was trying to portray to the world.

I wanted to be true to who I was, to attract real connections. Connection is what humans live and die for. Without it, we create disconnection in our society. We all need to take time to evaluate what our disconnections are and how we avoid using them to distance ourselves from our path. It could be your saving grace. I know for a fact that it was mine.

> **I wanted to be true to who I was, to then attract real connections. Connection is what humans live and die for. Without it, we create numbing in our society.**

We have become a society that quits when things get hard. Kids quit, couples quit, people press delete and block at the sign of the slightest storm. The instant gratification that we have buried ourselves in via technology and the idea of, "It needs to feel good right now," is killing us. Human evolution doesn't happen in thirty seconds or less. Our impatience is driving us to marry before we're ready, divorce before we're ready, sever relationships before we're ready.

Technology is the greatest form of escape and disconnection currently in our culture. As we scroll through the pages of social media, day by day, we begin to dissociate with the people and things around us. Whether we notice it or not, we also begin to compare ourselves with the posts, captions, and videos we absorb in the hours we spend on our phones. Rather than taking the moments by ourselves to sit, reflect, and meditate for a moment to think about the things we need to work on to better ourselves, we reach too quickly for our devices. I am guilty of doing this also. However, as I have embarked on this rediscovery of myself and my body, heart, mind, and soul, I have become more aware of how I can avoid these disconnections. From alcohol to my iPhone, I've decided that I will no longer allow myself to use these numbing vessels to escape whatever I may face day by day, morning through

"Peace, in its most fundamental form, is the connection of one human spirit to another."

— Archbishop Desmond Tutu

How can we create more connection?

night. I have chosen the path of reconnection between Source, self, others, and life. You can too.

Each of us has the agency to do this, to choose to bridge our true selves with the version of who we are in the present moment. We get to choose to connect and not disconnect from our path and purpose. It is hard a lot of the time to sit and be still. To sit and think. To sit and feel the good, the bad, and everything laced in between. It's not a simple journey to deal with the things in our past, present or future that haunt us, the things that we'd rather silence with alcohol, drugs, sex, food, technology, and all other forms of disconnections. Choosing to give yourself the chance to even try to face your fears, doubts, and worries is so *brave*. You deserve to be brave for yourself and no one else. Not your partner, parents, or people on social media— but for you. The question we all need to be asking is: *Why am I disconnected, and what am I afraid of?* Brené Brown has taught: "At the root of shame is the fear of disconnection or a loss of connection." We're all afraid of something. The loss of interaction above everything, but to know how to better connect with souls all seeking the same thing is one of the greatest seeds we could plant in our garden.

To create pockets of hope along the way, I schedule little things for myself; I consider them simple ways to help my garden flourish as I embark on the journey each day: journaling, focused meditation, retreats, life time-outs, walks through nature, all of it is designed to get in touch with my authentic self.

So get up. Make your bed. Do a thing, do another thing, do another thing. Do something self-soothing. Write. Do something kind for someone. Make a cookie. Make a phone call. Every hour do something. When you feel sad, weep and sob it out. Let the emotions flow in and out of your body naturally. When you disconnect, you block that natural flow that has to happen to remain healthy and aligned with, mind, body, and soul.

Don't curl up in bed. Don't go into a ball. Don't close off. Don't dive into your technology. Don't go away. Because as soon as you go away, you disconnect. And disconnection will put us in the darkest places all by ourselves until we don't have a reason to live—our own hell on Earth.

Connection starts with us. It starts with eye-to-eye contact—our very own windows to the soul. It starts with a no electronics zone. It starts with quality time dedicated to the person we are connecting with, including ourselves. We all want to know we are important, and multitasking does not tell anyone, someone else nor yourself, that you are there for them.

Q HOW TO BE HAPPY

> **Once we are there for the person we are communicating with, we become part of their Source and their soul where true connection and relationship begins.**

Pure joy is the result. We all want to be connected; our teenage years are rough getting through the peer-pressure phase of life. Some of us are still held in this phase of life.

In the end, your beautiful and most sacred body made up of all the scars that have been etched in your skin, the tears that have been collected over time, and the burning sensation of deep pain you have felt within your chest are all a part of you and your journey. They have reminded you of where you have been and the things you have survived.

One morning while I was having coffee with a family member who has suffered through addiction, they said to me, "I try to be an open book, and I try to be honest

" I define connection as the energy
that exists between people when they feel
seen, heard, and valued;
when they can give and receive without judgment;
and when they derive sustenance and
strength from the relationship."

—Brené Brown

because there is no holding back. That's what helps me, hearing someone else's story, knowing that they got through hard things. The rehab material . . . you can read through it all, but when it doesn't resonate with you, you skip over it. I can read and hear it, but another person's story who has been where I am now . . . that gives me hope that I can get through it too."

In true connection, it's easy when it's easy. Learning to work through it when it is hard—and be willing to be open and share who you truly are on your journey—is the challenge we all face. Every time I face judgements, I want to put up masks and boundaries to protect myself, but as soon as I do, nobody gets in to meet the real me.

> **We've got to accept the harsh reality that each day we are going to encounter judgments from all sorts of directions.**

We'll step out of our doors and begin to walk on the peace path, but then we'll get blindsided by something that is called guilt, shame, gay, straight, or whatever the label is being tossed at us that day. And from here, we get blasted to another path that puts us on the crash course with no direction.

When you get hit by shame, betrayal, or abandonment, it disorients you. You start asking yourself, *Where am I?*

Like a daisy blown in the wind, I have felt like pieces of me are everywhere. A piece of me is somewhere in the world with my lover, another piece wants to be in Heaven with my dad and gran, another piece is in the past, another is in the place I exist, and so on and so forth. And I ask myself, *So what is that? Is that disconnection, or is that connection to everything that is a part of me?*

The answer? *It is everything.* We keep wanting to have this beautiful little path called life, but it is messy and icky at times, overflowing with weeds and flowers. It's a mass awakening and an explosion back to self. The journey of enlightenment is when we learn how to understand that sometimes the body is here, our heart is in another place, the mind and soul are floating around somewhere else, and it's okay. You're not crazy. You're just trying to get on the path of purpose . . . hell, we all are.

Instead of feeling panicked and choosing not to listen to the voices, just try to be still. Let the energy that is trying to speak to you, speak. Listen. Everything that happens around us is destined to create separation, and everyone just wants to curl up in a ball and go away. However, the voices are messengers, so if you hear, see, or feel them, grab a journal, write, and don't edit. Remember the mask you made earlier? As you are processing your feelings, look back at your new masks, reflect and write on how you painted the new beliefs, attitudes, and ideas for your future higher self.

When we avoid reaching out for our disconnections, we give ourselves a chance to survive the pain and anguish and come out stronger than before. Every misstep we experience in life, we have the option to get back up and reach for true healing instead of the wrong sources.

I have had many great teachers who have taught me the path to great peace and happiness, including the way out of my victim mentality. Thank you to Dr. Brené Brown, Dr. Wayne Dyer, Marianne Williamson, Gabrielle Bernstein, Oprah, Eckhart Tolle, and Don Miguel Ruiz. I believe these mentors have brought universal inspiration and hope to my life.

Before taking the time to walk through my flowers or weeds, I was always angry, pissed, and closed off. I created a lack of vulnerability, loneliness, and abandonment and sabotaged so many significant relationships. I tried to drink it away, sex it away, run it away, work it away, eat it away—I tried everything to deny true emotion. The journey to pure love and forgiveness for ourselves and others is not a quick fix. It is not an overnight trip from point A to point B, but rather a series of short trips through different decades of our lives. Everything on our journey is a knowing of wisdom that you simply cannot get without walking the path.

What all of us as teachers are trying to say to you is that you can look at your life right now and decide that you are not your guilt, shame, or abandonment. Somebody else was guilty for hurting you, but you are not guilty. Don't be afraid to tell your story. Don't be ashamed that you were hurt or forsaken. Don't be afraid to talk about it. It is okay. We need to learn how to step onto the path of vulnerability, walk into the darkness, and find the light. All of us can do this.

It takes a lot of bravery to endure the terrible tribulations we must go through. It takes even more bravery to reach out for help instead of straying off the path to seek disconnection from reality. Sometimes we fall, and it's hard not to choose to hide from the darkness we deal with internally and externally. We get to stand up, cry hard, yell, and ask for help and understanding because nothing about being broken is weak or wrong. All of us are spirit beings having this human experience. We're all walking on different paths, but ultimately we're journeying toward the same goal, whether we believe that or not.

Whoever you are, wherever you are, please choose to be brave. Choose healing over hurting. Choose yourself, because when it is all said and done, our bodies are our homes here on Earth. Our paths are our journeys that lead us to serenity. Regardless of where you are right now—our life journeys, hills, valleys, mountains, and streams. We endure the storms on the way to sunny beaches, true love, and relationships on fire with connections we all can attract and create. Heaven on Earth is truly possible, and I am here to show you!

We get to choose connection and reconnection with the people, places, and things that give us joy, peace, and love, over and over and over again until we become the best versions of ourselves. We get to rebuild with the beautiful and broken pieces that shape us. We get to become who we were meant to be as we rejuvenate within the walls of our home, as we step out into the world time and time again, as we embark through this path we call life.

Lesson Five

No Technology Zone

Purpose: Why do 60 million Americans report that isolation and loneliness are major sources of unhappiness? There is a long history of data that suggest our technologies disconnect us from human relationships. Technology allows us to choose isolation over face-to-face contact. With this in mind, we encourage you to take the seven-day technology challenge.

Lesson: Remember your thoughts become your things. Over the next seven days, make your technology a manifesting machine of wants and desires. Relationships and true connection will be built; communication skills will be developed to open opportunities to share deeply meaningful life events that need and deserve connection.

Tools:
- Technology bin
- Sticky notes
- Puzzle
- Cards
- Favorite book
- Board games

Activity: Challenge yourself to limit technology.

step one:
Monday: Begin this challenge with yourself, family, or friends. Start with placing technology devices in a bin for a few hours each evening. I recommend using a plastic bin for group gatherings. Encourage all family members to delete negative content, and unfollow/unsubscribe from anything disconnecting, violent, or mean-spirited. If it doesn't have an uplifting, inspirational, or positive impact on your life, click Delete.

step two:
Tuesday: Have friends who come over drop their shoes at the door along with their cell phones in the technology device bin. Encourage kids to do a puzzle, paint, or play cards or a board game. Your home will become the place all the kids want

to hang out at. If you're single, challenge yourself to date without technology. On dates, make it a point to put the phones away, and work through the uncomfortable silence toward authentic connection. Remember, eyes are the window to the soul, so get eye contact from the person you are communicating with—you will know what they really think and believe.

step three:
Wednesday: Charge your phone at night anywhere but your bedroom and stay away from it starting at least two hours before bed! Read a book, not a link. Find two-hour blocks daily to walk away from your phone.

step four:
Thursday: Write a daily gratitude and put one manifesting thought from your dream board front and center on a sticky note.

step five:
Friday: Go out in the evening and be social. Challenge all your friends to not engage with their phones while you are together. The first person to look at their phone has to buy dinner or drinks.

step six:
Saturday: Don't look at or post anything on social media.

step seven:
Sunday: Switch your phone off for the entire day. Make your morning coffee or tea, and reflect on the week. Write or speak out loud about how you feel and what you have noticed are areas for change in the following week. Pick one thing that you feel needs to be addressed for a better you. Thank it for appearing to you so clearly. Write or mediate about the future state you will experience when you let this feeling, thought, or emotion go.

(5)

Our Transformations

2007—the year I almost died.

I was in Mexico on one of my life's time-out retreats with some of my best friends when we decided to go on a scuba diving excursion. Our dive was for about an hour at an amateur level of less than fifty feet. It was truly a magnificent experience, swimming in a wonderful array of colors below the water's surface. It was like nothing I'd ever experienced before. After the dive, my group took me out for my birthday dinner, but the celebration had been cut short because I began to feel a horrific headache coming on.

I thought it was due to so much fun and sun during the day or perhaps a mild case of dehydration. I turned in early to ease my headache but could not sleep most of the night. I awoke the next morning to more uneasiness, but I decided to ignore it, and I continued to pack for our trip back home. Upon checking in at the airport, my condition worsened, and the gate agents were not sure if they could allow me on the flight due to their concern that I may have had the bends—a decompression sickness scuba divers may experience if they ascend too rapidly from deep water.

I assured them that I was fine, and that I only needed to get back to Salt Lake City to recover. Moments later, I found myself walking into the confines of the airplane. An action that I would soon regret. As our flight took off, the air pressure magnified by headache to an excruciating level of pain. By the time we landed, they had a wheelchair waiting for me at the jet bridge.

I was taken to the hospital where doctors diagnosed my pain to be a severe migraine. They gave me a shot and sent me home. By the next day, I began to feel better, and I traveled to Pocatello, Idaho, to attend a meeting for USA Volleyball. As I got up to speak at the presentation, I began to lose feeling in my extremities, and I felt tingling everywhere. Everything went black, and I woke up in a nearby hospital's hyperbaric chamber.

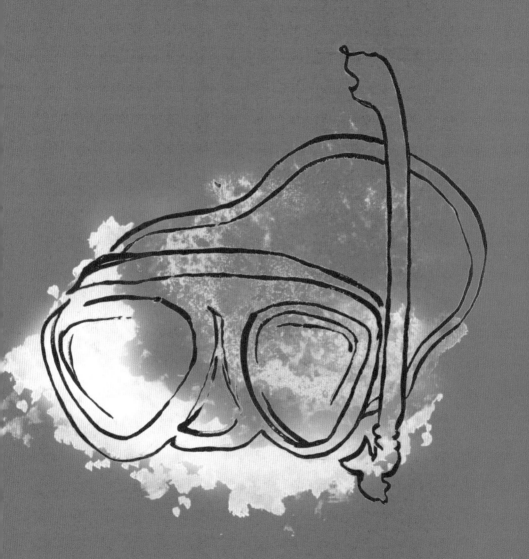

This chamber allowed doctors to return my body to below-sea-level pressure. This provided them with the needed time to confirm I was suffering from carbon monoxide poisoning. Just before I woke up and saw my sobbing parents through the chamber windows, doctors told them I was as near death as one could get without actually dying.

The timing of these events from Mexico to Idaho could not have been anything less than divine design. The hyperbaric chamber saved my life. Had I not traveled that day to Pocatello, Idaho, for that coaching clinic, I would not have had access to the only hyperbaric chamber that side of the Rocky Mountains. That miracle is why I am here today writing of this experience. God truly works in mysterious ways.

I think back to that dark and terrifying time, and how the tender mercies of life often work in our own favors without us even realizing it.

Within all the disarray of everything whirling around me, the voices of doctors, the ambient noise of machines, the voices of people who cared about me, I distinctly remember my angel grandmother came to me. I experienced it all, the white light, the feeling of floating, the pure bliss of Heaven . . . and I begged her to take me with her. I was ready to go. Instead, she told me no, and that I needed to go back and change the world.

My near-death experience, and my stepbrother's suicide the following month, launched me like a rocket into my new mission: to change the world. What I learned on this personal journey of transformation is that when you change your world, the world changes. So, I started my personal journey of transformation.

I decided the excess weight had to go. I had to heal my body and heal my life, so I did. I got a lap band surgery to help me lose weight, and I lost over one hundred pounds. At this point in my life, I was experiencing great success and happiness with my businesses, coaching career, and girlfriend, who I thought was the love of my life. I had just built my dream home, was driving my coveted Mercedes-Benz, and was considered successful in all dimensions of my life. I thought I had achieved it all.

Despite all the wonderful things that were happening, I was still longing for something that was hidden beyond the protective mask of fat. My invisible soul was seeking transformation on the inside; my soul wanted to be accepted in its own skin for who and what she was. The years of fear, shame, betrayal, and abandonment bubbled to the surface demanding their time, attention, and love. Success could no longer fill these voids.

To the outside world, I portrayed the image of a tough, cocky, powerful woman. On the inside, I was lonely, afraid, and ashamed of who I was as a gay Christian. How could God love me? The mask I wore looked like success in business, coaching, and life, but it was also what kept intimacy, affection, and love far away. As the masks and the weight started to come down, my confidence in myself started to come up because there was no way both of those elements of myself were going to survive together. As one was dying, another was emerging.

It was a time when I was replanting things along my path, taking full advantage of the lessons being presented to me. As people noticed my mask of weight slipping away, they were constantly telling me how great I looked. It felt good, but other times it felt scary, messy, and hard. Each time I had these feelings I wrote about them; I explored their roots and began to establish the *why* of so many feelings I had buried alive.

The weeds (buried emotional pain bodies) were being set into a new planter so that I could plant new ideas, feelings, and joy in my old planter. It was miraculous, beautiful, and loving; it was everything I wanted. My thoughts were going to be my things. It was the ever-changing love story of my life's transformation.

With all of these experiences behind me, I realized my purpose on Earth was to coach other souls to success by teaching them how to take old thoughts, replant them, and create new thoughts that would change their world. I created and implemented a 5 Step Path Forward System to coach souls to success. I started teaching others how to win the game of life. After almost losing my life, and my brother taking his own, I was determined to teach everyone I could how to live their best life.

I was transforming and living an amazing life. I felt I had beaten back the dark night of the soul and was headed toward life's easy street. Little did I know, God had a different plan in store for my life. Everything I had planted was going to die! I was going to experience death, loss, and letting go.

My dad was the first great loss, followed shortly thereafter by the loss of my company, and then being fired from my college coaching career. God had a plan, but I was devastated. I felt like I was drowning and could not figure out what to do. Gone were the physical weight and the emotional weight. Not only was I free of the body weight, but I was also now free of the business, the career, the home, and the car. I was fifty years old and starting over. I was scared, but I had been coaching

other souls to success, so I decided my path-forward system would need to be implemented in my own life. Twenty years of blood, sweat, and tears went up in flames within months. I knew God would never test me more than I could endure, so I asked Grace to replant my life with joy, love, peace, and the easy button.

Looking back on it all, the physical weight wasn't anything compared to the weight I was carrying inside and the blocks I continued to create on my path. As I have come to learn more about our first seeds, our masks, our judgements, our disconnections, and *Our Soul's Journey*—I understand that those were all heavy elements I had been carrying around my whole life. I wanted to become healthy and whole and experience people in a good space. You'll learn along the way that people who are truly with us on our journeys will always be there for us. No matter where you are, even if you feel completely alone, God will send us who or what is next to carry us through.

The path to recovery is daily asking, listening, seeking with Source, and following our guides to transformation of body, mind, and soul. Until I became connected again with my God and my Source, and I sought out wholehearted transformation through rediscovering *who I was* and *who I wanted to become* . . . I couldn't lose the excess pounds.

To my readers: you are going to have success and tears and will have to start over. But if we can all learn to consistently revisit our life's garden, weed, and plant over and over and again as we journey through our path, we will all understand ourselves better. The dream board is both *who we are* and *who we want to become*. It is the past, present, and future, and it is the map that we can use to get from here to there. *Transformation* and *experience* could be the same word. Without the experience of

success, we don't know where we come from, and without the experience of failure, we don't know what we can do. In the journey to true transformation, the experience will only build you for that moment to prepare you for the trials that will come again. The difference is as we get older, we gain wisdom and scars, and those scars remind us that as much as we've been bruised and defeated, we will find success on the other side.

> **Transformation and experience could be the same word. Without the experience of success, we don't know where we come from and without the experience of failure, we don't know what we can do.**

There must come a time in everyone's life when you realize that enough is enough. That carrying around the weight of who we let others think we are versus who we truly are is no longer worth it. Sooner or later, we miss who we were before we let the poison destroy our miraculous gardens. Somewhere behind the masks we portray to the world, within us is just a child who had dreams of their own. Beyond our judgements of ourselves and others, we were only seeking meaning behind the facades we put up. Aside from the disconnections we put ourselves through with alcohol, drugs, sex, money, or food, the only thing we need to silence or numb is the disbelief in ourselves.

Beyond what the world sees, it is only the *belief in ourselves* that truly matters.

In the end, the ultimate desire of *our transformation* flows within us. You, me, and our Sources. One body, mind, and spirit are all perfectly whole here on Earth.

"It is a strange and wonderful fact to be here, walking around in a body, to have a whole world within you and a whole world at your fingertips outside you."

—John O'Donohue

Lesson Six
Manifest Your Life Forward

Purpose: Manifesting yourself into the future should have a high vibration of energy and excitement. It doesn't matter how far in the future you decide to manifest forward, but it does matter that you start *now*! Dream your soul to success; don't let one ounce of doubt or limitation creep into your dream. Clear away anything you do not want in your life by writing about what you deserve.

Tools:
- Journal
- Pen
- Paper

Activity: Manifest your dream life.

step one:
Start with a piece of paper. Draw a line down the middle of the page. At the top of column one write: *I DESERVE*. At the top of column two write: *I CLEAR*.

step two:
Under the *I DESERVE* column, write everything you deserve to have in life, each time resistance is felt or thought of, write that feeling or thought in the *I CLEAR* column.

step three:
After you have completed your *I DESERVE* column, write the following letter to God or your Source, "My life is so amazing and wonderful now that I have accomplished _____." Write as if everything in the *I DESERVE* column is your present reality.

Return to this exercise regularly to remind yourself of the direction you're heading.

Part Two

For Our Hearts

Our Mountains, Peaks, and Valleys

If life has taught me anything, it is that there are highs and lows in every moment we are alive. We know from EKG readings that when the line is flat, there is no life. So, to understand why we must all suffer through heartache, emotional distress, and everything laced through it all, we enter the journey through the Mountains, Peaks, and Valleys of Our Hearts.

Chapters

---

(6)

Our True Loves

If Mount Everest were a person, its name would be Bob Norman—also known as my dad. His philosophy to live and love life at its highest elevation has been one of my greatest examples.

My dad taught me that everything is energy and to give energy to what you want most of all, to what you *love*. He knew the perfect love of Christ, God's grace, and undeserved favor. He knew that emotions are choices. That no one and nothing makes you happy. *Happiness is your choice, so always enjoy your life.*

> **"No one and no thing makes you happy. Happiness is your choice, so always enjoy your life." —Bob Norman**

My dad knew about family; he knew much more than I ever understood. He taught me that we are all related, that everyone is family, and that there was no difference between us.

My dad was a giver; he was not a fighter. He was slow to anger. He was not a gossip, never blamed others, and was always responsible for his choices. He knew that forgiveness was a gift of grace we all deserve. Every day when my dad dropped me off at school, he would say to me, "Do something kind today." Through giving, loving, caring, and sharing, he taught me that acts of kindness change the world.

Serotonin is a chemical released in the brain when a person witnesses an act of kindness. Studies have shown that the giver receives double doses of this chemical. No wonder my dad was legally high . . . on life, for this was the way he lived it. My dad was a creator, an artist, a jokester, a lover, and a flirt. He would always say to the ladies, "You are so beautiful." Later in life, he would then follow by saying, "I am legally blind."

(I L O V E Y O U)

Through my dad, I learned that hard work is how we learn pride, joy, and self-love. He was always so excited to live life, and he had high energy while doing it. He took up snow skiing at age sixty, started a water park at age seventy, and rode the UTV late into his eighties. My brothers could tell you that he was infamous for water skiing with his ball hat and a cigar at his lips. He had a huge crash once, and we were afraid he was hurt. Instead, he came out of the water with the hat and cigar all in one. I have never met a man who worked so hard. He did not know what being bored was, and he taught me that the job was never done unless it was done well. He was so fun to be around, and he was the life of every party. He had a joke for everything in life. He really knew how to make your heart smile, and if any of you reading this has someone like my dad in your life, hold onto them dearly.

Like any elderly person, my dad didn't know about texts, emails, or cell phones, and yet, he was an extraordinary communicator. He had deaf parents, and he knew that 95 percent of communication is nonverbal. Even in the last hours of his life, he was signing, "I love you," to us all. He did not need the spoken word to show love.

My dad knew about relationships, and he taught me that each one took time, love, compassion, and non-judgement. He knew that everyone was on their life's journey and love was the blessing that should always be sent. The scripture I Corinthians 13:13 ("And now abideth faith, hope, love these three; but the greatest of these is love") was a classic example of what my dad believed.

> **The scripture, I Corinthians 13:13 says, "And now abideth faith, hope, and love, these three; but the greatest of these is love," was what my dad believed.**

My daddy's life was a celebration of living, giving, and loving all. My wish for you and for me is that we take his life as an example to live ours with purpose. I am thankful every day that he walks with me, not ahead, and not behind, but beside me, for I know he is always with me. This part of the book is dedicated to my dad, my first true love.

Six Daily Reminders from My Dad

Purpose: To experience being high on life through acts of kindness. When we practice acts of kindness, our bodies will naturally release serotonin. Witnessing acts of kindness creates the same effects. Our lesson is about creating every opportunity life offers you to create daily doses of a serotonin high.

Tools:
- A quiet space
- Journal
- Pen
- Paper

"Every act of love is a work of peace no matter how small."

— Mother Teresa

Activity: Recite mantras to yourself.

step one:
Remember who you are as you leave your house each day. What you meet your day with is what you create. Create acts of kindness.

step two:
Don't take things personally. If someone is creating anger, try to create peace. Take a minute to ask that person if they are okay or if they need to be heard, seen, or given a hug.

step three:
When you begin to tell yourself you are not enough, tell five people how amazing they are and how much you love and care about them.

step four:
Believe in the change you create in the world. Pick up a few pieces of trash, offer to help someone open their door, or clean up something without being asked.

step five:
Take some time each day to write about why you think another person's opinion is so wrong. Write it as though you are them and they are you. This will likely bring you more understanding and tolerance. Respect is one of the greatest expressions of love.

step six:
Write a personal love letter to yourself. Express the devotion you are extending to your soul. Place it in a safe space near your bed and read it on those nights you find really difficult to find peace.

This activity will assist you in creating the natural high from serotonin. By giving gratitude and grace to others through acts of kindness, you reciprocally give loving kindness to yourself.

(7)

Our Heartaches

My aspiration is to live life as if every moment was at the top of the peak, but many times I have found myself trapped in the valley of heartache and sorrow. I'm certain you have too. If you've followed my lessons so far with building and creating a dream board, then like me, you've probably plastered a picture of you and your lover on it. If you didn't, well congratulations, you don't have to struggle with the decision to tear or not tear the picture off the board when you hit relationship lows with them. Yes, my dad taught me about unconditional love, but I had to learn about the lesson of heartache on my own. So, trust me when I say, I too have known the pain of drifted love between another soul and myself.

You know those moments, days, or months after a bad breakup? The times when your heart is hurting so bad that you would do anything to try and numb the pain? We have all hit those roadblocks along our path called life, and they suck. We try to keep it together while moving forward, but honestly, it is so much harder to say than to do.

For me, I've always had people say, "You're so strong. You've got this. Move on. You're going to be okay," and I wonder, *Well, when? When am I going to feel okay again?* Because honestly, my day could be going fine and then boom . . . a memory hits. Or bam . . . something I see or hear reminds me of them. I'm constantly trying to hold it together and move forward, but the only way I feel is scattered. We've all been through it. Maybe not the same way, but I know that everyone experiences times when you just don't know where to go. Up or down, right or left. The pathway could be split into a thousand directions, and I would still not know whether to turn around or just push forward. The EKG line might as well become flat, because yes, heartbreaks could be life-ending catalysts.

Of course all while this is happening, I struggled to keep it all together. My emotional state could be compared to items in a well-used hiking backpack: scattered, broken,

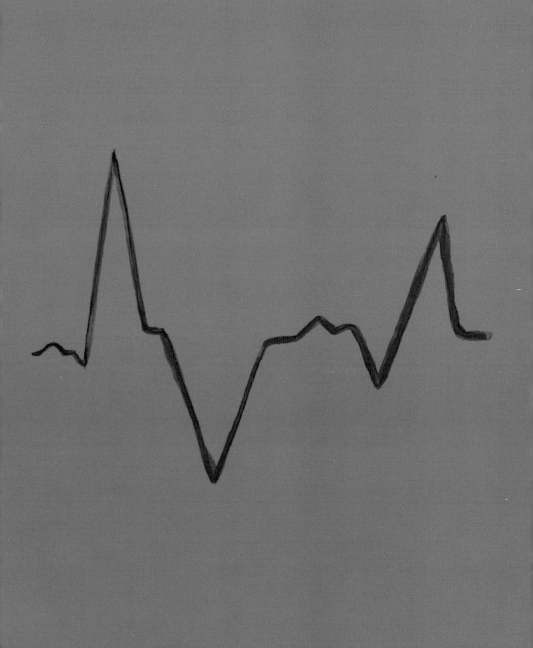

some parts useful, most parts numb, but all still essential elements needed for our survival in the wilderness. The bag keeps things manageable as you embark on your hike and journey through the highs and lows of the terrain etched in your heart.

Let's take a second to visualize what these feelings would look like. Imagine yourself in a canyon. Now, imagine that your backpack tears, releasing everything inside onto the ground. Now you have to carry all of it in your hands. Instead of taking a moment to stop, reassess, and fix your backpack, you rush to continue forward. As you walk along the rocky path, searching for a way out of the canyon, you notice that you've dropped valuable things, and a trail of broken parts and pieces lay behind you.

You pause and try to hold everything else in your arms, while at the same time struggling to reach for the pieces that fell. Some of you may be smart enough by now to put everything down and fix what needs to be fixed. But if you're like me, you would just struggle harder to snag the pieces that are on the floor nearest to you, while at the same time refusing to put anything down. Pretty soon, another precious piece falls, and another, and soon enough, your pile is just a messy bundle. You find yourself on the ground, collecting everything while trying to keep *yourself* together—you're tired, broken, and hurt.

It's like each of those pieces and parts could be compared to pieces of you. You're trying to move forward with the broken bits that are left, and you are trying to find the pieces that trailed behind. You feel scattered all over the path of life, wanting only that piece of your heart back to feel whole again.

> **While everything is falling apart, you forget that you have to heal to have the strength to find your way out of the canyon and valley—to pick up all the broken, abandoned, shattered pieces, get back up and continue to walk forward.**

This, my friend, is heartache. This is where we grow the most. The times in our life that we get to learn from, no matter how painful, no matter how hard. That's the mental war with our heart, mind, body, and soul. This constant internal battle that asks: *What's today going to be? Are we going to sit and sulk on the trail with all the shattered parts of us, or are we going to fix what needs stitching, hold the pieces all close, and get to our destination in one piece?*

"We all have a bag. We all pack differently. Some of us are traveling light. Some of us are secret hoarders who've never parted with a memory in our lives. I think we are all called to figure out how to carry our bag to the best of our ability, how to unpack it, and how to face the mess. I think part of growing up is learning how to sit down on the floor with all your things and figuring out what to take with you and what to leave behind."

–Hannah Brencher

"Risks can lead to great victories or defeats. Even if you are defeated, the lesson will be valuable for the next stage of life."

— Lailah Gifty Akita

It takes a warrior to overcome and win this emotional battle.

Nobody wakes up ready to embark on their journey, saying to themselves, *I am going to have heartache today*, because who in the hell would want to do that? Brené Brown's research shows that "when people believe themselves worthy of connection, they're more likely to move toward others. They'll be the first to say, 'I love you.' They'll be quick to say, 'I miss you' (not just in absence but in growing apart). They'll ask for help, and they'll be open to the love, affection, and influence of others. They'll be grateful. They'll be connected." If we are all seeking connection, and heartache is the natural bridge burner, then how do we use the painful energy to our advantage, rather than our destruction? The answer is to take each and every hurting experience and search for the lessons meant to help us grow stronger. Experiences, too, are seeds that we get to plant along the path we walk.

"We must go for it; play life with great courage and reckless abandon."

As Vernon Sanders Law says, "Experience is a hard teacher because she gives the test first, the lesson afterward." It's not easy, but it is reality. Failure is not to be feared. Pouring into all of life's opportunities is risky, but without the risk, the rewards will not be possible. We will never know the most beautiful moments meant for us to live without the absolute faith of free-falling in and out of love.

We must go for it; play life with great courage and reckless abandon. Regret is the one thing we all can do something about. When it comes to love, commitment, and golden relationships where you and another person can love and be loved effortlessly, so too comes the challenge of self-reflection and understanding. Take the necessary steps to seek what was amazing in your past and what changes you deserve to make for the future voyage.

This doesn't mean you'll always get your heart broken, but it does mean that when you are more willing to be open and vulnerable in relationships, your potential for shame is less. Even if the connection falls short—if the, "I love you," is left hanging, the "I miss you," isn't returned, the request for help is declined—you would know that it is just a part of the journey. Work to know that you can love and be loved unconditionally as you continue to give it out. People who believe they are worthy of connection are less likely to blame themselves and their own "unworthiness" for the disconnection. They are often the people who people want to be with. They give to the relationship and they receive it openly, abundantly, honestly, and with love and gratitude. They allow themselves to be vulnerable to the uncertainty, and they make it safe for others to do the same.

I am thankful for the intimate relationships I've shared and the lessons I have learned about life, love, and connection. To each of you (my former partners) reading this, I am humbly grateful for the heartbreak. I learned to love myself even deeper and to take the time to heal and find what was lost or broken along the trail. I am also thankful for the great teachers Dr. Brené Brown and Dr. Wayne Dyer for teaching that to continue to love deeply is not a weakness but a strength. I know that as my past partners moved on, my love for them created discomfort in the beginning, and some of them could not remain close. Choosing to give them all a choice, knowing that I could be unconditional love and show up if needed, has blessed my life greatly. Love, before, during, and after our soul's journey changed.

As we get to know people, we begin to judge the things that don't measure up instead of just loving them unconditionally. We will destroy the best things in our life when we have not dealt with our disconnectors. When we get closer to Source, truth, love, passion, and connection, the healing energy we emulate draws nearer to the souls that should journey with us. The people we are meant to be with.

> **"You see, in the final analysis, it is between you and your God. It was never between you and them anyway. —Mother Teresa**

In her poem "Final Analysis," Mother Teresa gives us great guidelines for life, and how to navigate our paths through heartache. To fully live our life's passion and purpose, we need to put it all *in*. For any endeavor to work, we need to commit. Commitment is easy when everything is going our way. Commitment, when challenged, is when people in relationships begin to look for the Delete button.

There was a time in history when the common belief was that divorce was not okay. I'm not saying that there is no good reason to move on from relationships that aren't working—especially abusive ones—but I do think that often we quit in the icky middle of healthier relationships without truly working for resolution and understanding. We must go into relationships with commitment and truly try to understand and heal, and if our partner doesn't choose us in the end or they don't respond, react, or do what we hoped, then it was never meant to be anyways.

That's the challenging part: understanding that if it it's not meant to be, it will never be. And that's okay, because there is someone out there for each of us. We need to be willing to risk, fail, learn, and try again. Every soul has a mate.

"People are often
unreasonable,
irrational, and
self-centered.
Forgive them anyway.

If you are kind,
people may accuse
you of selfish,
ulterior motives.
Be kind anyway.

If you are successful,
you will win some
unfaithful friends
and some genuine
enemies.
Succeed anyway.

If you are honest
and frank, people
may cheat you.
Be honest and frank
anyway.

What you spend years
building, someone
could destroy
overnight.
Build anyway.

If you find serenity
and happiness,
they may be jealous.
Be happy anyway.

The good you do
today, people will
often forget tomorrow.
Do good anyway.

Give the world the
best you have,
and it will never be
enough.
Give the best you've
got anyway.

In the final analysis,
it is between you and
God; it was never
between
you and them
anyway."

—Mother Teresa

When we experience heartaches, it is always difficult to pull ourselves back together and to get up and try again, but the resilient ones will always do this. Brokenhearted and all. After any breakup, we're constantly wrestling with vulnerability and asking ourselves all the time: *How much do I put in, say, or do?* We let our past heartaches determine the scale of how open, how reserved, or how careful we are with letting someone in. Instead, we have to learn that if we don't put ourselves out there, we will never know. The ultimate way to connect between us and another soul is vulnerability. If we want to be with them, we've got to lay it all out there, let it go, and let it flow, knowing that we are taking that risk of falling completely over the waterfall of love and heartache. With beauty comes pain, with blessing comes trial. None of us is going to find someone without first being real with who we are and what we want with no fears, shame, or expectations of the other person.

Most people are holding back and protecting themselves with their masks, but who is going to call bullshit and say, "Say what you feel, feel what you say, and really mean it!" This is one of my many goals—to just be an authentic lover. To share it and show it because it is who we are. We are love. We are joy. We are peace.

Gaining the strength again after encountering those moments of shattered pieces along the path is always going to be hard. To try and find the balance and inner peace of love, joy, and hope within us is a significant part of the journey to empowerment. It goes back to the moments when we are on the floor with the broken parts of us everywhere—the moments when we are struggling to gather it all back together and continue to fight to get to our destination in one piece. But it is in these pauses of our life that we have to take a second to look at what was broken inside or around us. These are the times we need to go deep inside of ourselves and find what is hurting. With every heartache comes the healing process, right? Rather than rushing through it just to get to the next part of our life, we get to take the time to heal and learn about who we are and the things we can endure to make us stronger.

It's okay to free-fall in love over and over again. We will learn things about ourselves from every relationship and every breakup. For me, I learned that I could go through a devastating separation and still come out of the canyon of heartache stronger than before. Instead of creating barriers that would never allow a future love to enter my life, I dove deep to ask myself: *What part of me is creating the barriers that would not allow the greatest love of my life? What thing within myself is not deserving?* When we can ask ourselves the hard questions, the answers will come. It is not a mystery.

Consider what you are pondering, and ask yourself: *Why is there a block?* When you let it be spoken, it is usually fear. You dove deep, and when it got too deep you began to put up the barrier. The honest to God truth is that I did the same thing. It wasn't about your partner, and it wasn't about mine. We fooled ourselves to think we were all in, and when it was getting too committed, instead of letting go and being free, we sabotaged it, and the question is: *Why?* When I finally had the courage to seek and find the answers, I did not feel worthy to deserve the love that another person was trying to give me. Until we can go into it and ask ourselves, *Where did this fear come from? Where did it get embedded? Where did that feeling get buried alive, at what age?* we won't find the solution to our problems.

Throughout my lifetime, I was the common denominator in the reasons for why every relationship had not worked out. Take away the name of my first partner from when I was twenty-one, or the one after that, or even the one after that...the story was the same. And who wrote that story? I did. It was a new character, but it was the same script.

It takes time to know how to fix any and every part of us that needs healing. I had to do this in order to not only stitch myself back together, but also to become the best version of me to then attract the best version of love back into my life. To have two people's lives, lived on purpose, that intertwine together so that Source's purpose works through both of them, not one or the other, but together, that is the ultimate goal of *Our Soul's Journey*.

As soon as I realized this, the game changed. This is why I decided to write this book and go into life coaching because of my passion to teach the world what was learned through my own trials and tribulations. Pull back the veil of abandonment, fear, shame, expectation, and judgement to see what is in the way of our best relationships, our best lives. There are hints and clues sprinkled within every lesson that is sent to us, from our lovers, friends, family, coworkers, and everyone in between.

Yes, it would be so much easier to try and rush the process and take their picture off the dream board instead of taking the time to search for the lessons within each heartbreak. Go the distance, look at ourselves first before looking at them and what they did. Blaming the other person for that pain will only cause more hurt, more fear, more false expectations of the next one who comes along and tries to love us.

And that's the challenge, right? To not break and run, but instead take a peek into our untapped sources, absorb each and every angel lesson that is sent for us to learn, and mend our own hearts. Choose the path back to self-discovery and understanding to learn about our greatest peaks and valleys, to know the way out from a canyon of heartache.

"Wherever you go, go with all your heart."

—Confucius

What heartaches do you need to heal from?

Lesson Eight
Risk & Repeat

Purpose: Practice failing epically today. Your job is to fail at least one time today. Take at least one action today that puts you at risk for rejection. Make that call, or tell someone the thing you've had on your chest for a long time. Whatever you choose, make it a risk. Say yes to requests that stretch you personally and emotionally today. If the risk is clearly not in your best interests, then don't do it. However, if it is, go for it. Consciously remind yourself throughout the day you can do anything, and failure is not fatal.

Be the creator of your life. When we are in heartache or distress, the strategy is to not let the waterfall take you over. We are going to do everything as human beings to survive and avoid being plummeted to the bottom by reaching for a buoy that someone may throw or trying to swim upstream. The victim mindset would motivate us to just blame the water for flowing too fast and give up. This is a lesson of flipping how you are looking at a situation to become the creator of your own risks and failures. We need to be able to say to ourselves, *I am not going to just let go and die at the hands of the falls.* A growth mindset would choose to grab a rock, swim to the side, or jump out beyond the rocks to the deep part of the waterfall pool below. The story is not over. The solution is taking the risk.

Tools
- Journal
- Pen

Activity: Rewrite your story.

step one
Take out your journal and write a list of all the risks you have not taken and actions you have been avoiding in your search for love or accomplishing goals.

step two
Complete the following questions with as many answers as are true for you.
- What role did I play in my victim story?
- How can I take the role I played and change my life?

step three

From these answers, please do the following:

First, own the story you have written up to this point—you are not the victim. Write the story from the victim's role, how you perceived it.

Second, rewrite the same story, but tell it from how you wanted it to end, change, or how you would have done it differently. You will be surprised at what you create next.

You can use this exercise for any frustrating or heartbreaking situation you've been carrying with you. Keep your exercises with you, and when you encounter hard moments when you start sinking back into that victim mentality, return to your answers to lift yourself out of that darkness.

(8)

Our Relationships

In Utah, there are beautiful trails that you can hike through. Many of them interlace throughout the Rocky Mountains. Oftentimes, as you walk through these pathways, you may come across bridges that connect one side to the other. Our relationships could be compared to this metaphorical or even physical crossing of the bridge that gets you from one place to the next.

Relationships that last have a few common threads:

> ## Truthfulness, forgiveness, and unconditional love.

My dog Taylor was a beautiful illustration of these qualities each day. Upon returning home, Taylor was always at the ready. Ready to be in a relationship with me or to return to her own bidding if I was not in the mood or able to rub her belly, take a walk, or grab her food. She didn't get frustrated or began to rehearse ideas in her head around how I must be feeling. She was just there, ready and excited to be in a relationship with me, but she was also just as happy going about her dog life of unconditional love, so pure and ever flowing. Taylor passed away this year, and though she is gone, I know that her angel spirit walks beside me each day.

When we know what we need and want, the real question is how can we find our partners and relationships that are unconditional love, like my golden retriever Taylor? The answer to these questions begins with us.

When we maintain responsibility for our own happiness, true love continues. The moment I expect my partner to make me happy, the relationship starts down a slippery slope, right back into a canyon. Each day, two people must learn to come to a partnership with 100 percent of their best selves. We need to work on ourselves, not work on changing others. Learning to love flaws, holding space for other people

"While we cry ourselves
to sleep,
gratitude waits
patiently
to console and
reassure us;
there is a
landscape larger
than one
we can see."

—Sarah Ban Breathnach

and their imperfections, creating the tolerance to let others do their life their way—that is love.

To love someone unconditionally is hard, because to truly love them means to say, "My goodness, I love you, and I will love you as you pursue your own path and journey. Good luck. I will pray for you, I will be here for you, even if that means you can't or won't be here for me." That, to me, is the definition of a real relationship because I am coming to you with unconditional love, in pure support that your life's journey be perfect with or without me.

The night my partner told me she was leaving was filled with natural knowing, devastation, and peace. My spirit knew the night before during my full moon release that something big was going to fly into my life. Little did I know that big thing was actually something that was going to fly away. The human part of me was shattered, broken, and afraid of being alone. It was going to be difficult, because I truly believed that this woman was a part of my life's work here on Earth. I had become so pleasantly dependent on our relationship that I wasn't seeking God's plan for my life.

I was feeling passionless and not completely happy with the direction of my life, but I was not unhappy meeting the needs of our relationship. I thought we would both seek and find our passion and purpose together, because I absolutely loved this woman and was willing to accept a lot of things because she was truly important to me. My need for deep connection and belonging with an amazing, empathic person outweighed anything else. I also knew I would seek deep understanding to change the relationship direction with her rather than choosing to disconnect. Not choosing emotions of anger and hate to get over heartbreak is extremely difficult because we are in pain, and many of our past wounds of betrayal, abandonment, and shame rear their ugly heads. These are the times of great opportunity to create big personal transformations. Continue working on self while allowing God to refine us toward our purpose and passion. I chose love and compassion for this angel, because we both deserve it. This has been the best thing I have ever done.

Yes, it would have been so much easier for me to just walk away. To just shift to the space I was in, and say, "I am pissed at you. Take all your things from the house. Get the fuck out, and don't ever call me again; we're not friends." But now, as I am learning more about love and myself, I realized those thoughts, feelings, and words were the protective poison that I sprinkled along my own path. These actions would keep the true love of my life from coming in and planting her flowers. Healthy soil is needed to grow.

Eventually, with the help of a life coach, I opened my heart. I was finally strong enough to say, "You know, I don't need you. I want you, but I don't need you. So, wherever you must go, go. I will always be here for you."

Since the breakup, I have had an absolute reset with myself and people around me, because now there is no expectation with anyone who comes in and out of my path other than an opportunity to connect. Source and truth are one. I have been honest about my intentions, desires, and journey of life with all who come into my presence. I have requested that they show their true selves without expectation, judgement, or fear. How fun it has been to truly connect, communicate, and expect nothing but love.

To connect is easier than we make it seem. Sometimes it's just about being genuine, vulnerable, and willing to walk across the bridge of friendship. My goal is to create a lot of wonderful relationships that are unconditional love that say, "I am here for you. In the middle of the night, if you need a friend, call me. Let's talk through it. Let's argue. Let's disagree. Let's get in a fight and still be friends," because that is where real relationships are formed.

True relationships are the friendships that refuse to break. No one can tell me that they don't want belonging or deep connection. It is the greatest desire of every soul that walks the planet, because humans are pack mammals. We do not do well alone. Cultures and species have known that you need connection to survive. The human soul wants a tribe that loves it and will take the risk of crossing the bridge when it gets difficult.

Oftentimes we believe that the journey to our souls is *disconnection*, when in fact it's *connection*. We talk about boundaries and barriers, when in reality, relationships are built when we can figure out the blocks that are challenging our relationships. These are the moments that open up the opportunity for growth within us. Some of the biggest ways to get through boundaries and overcome disconnection is with each other.

> **Some of the biggest ways to get through boundaries and overcome disconnection is with each other—to really try and build through the good and bad, and always do it together.**

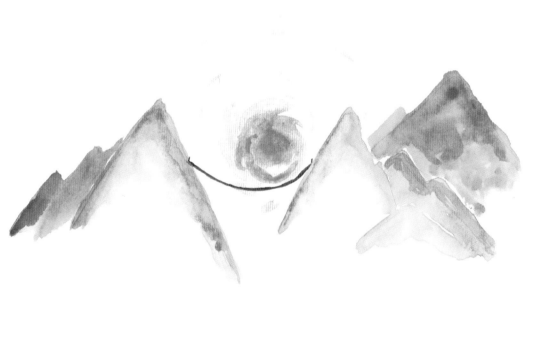

My father taught me that nobody ever builds alone; we are all interconnected. He was always creating to care for others—especially for his family and his friends. He would've given you the shirt on his back over and over again, and he was truly the most generous human being. Once again, his example was beyond comprehension. This life that I have created, destroyed, and built over again and again has been a symphony of ups and downs. I've learned through everything that relationships with the people we love most in our lives also get sifted through this yin and yang of good and bad; there is a constant battle trying to find balance.

We know when we want to be with another person, we are willing to do things we wouldn't do for anybody else. Genuine relationships between people are also the yin and yang of give and take. It's important that our partners know we are totally capable of standing on our own two feet, but we are also able to be in full support of their journey.

It is crucial that couples, regardless of their sexual orientation, learn how to manage their lives both separate and together. In relationships, it gets hard if I can't deal with both my own life and my partner's life. When this happens, we can't deal with *our* life. That's what pulls us apart, not only from ourselves, but from the people we love. Somewhere along the line, everyone is trying to find themselves and *us*. By *us* I mean them and their partner joined together. If every day you and I are loving that person unconditionally, willing to learn and grow to get to tomorrow, then we will have an eternity of tomorrows.

The question we must constantly be asking ourselves and the people we seek to be in relationships with should be: *What's good for you? What's good for me?* When we can consider this together, we can merge our paths and plant the seeds along the way. Who knows what we will grow. In this healthy scenario, I want to be able to say, "I love you so much that whatever we want to do is fulfilling to you and I both." It has to be a mutual asking of: *What's on your dream board? What's on mine? How do we merge?*

I have to dream my dream, and see if the person I love is dreaming their dream, and then make sure it all matches up. You must do the same. We all need to find the balance between what they love and what we love. We need to learn how to make sacrifices and exceptions to keep our relationships balanced. We are working toward a perfect blend of yin and yang, ups and downs, rights and wrongs, bridges, boundaries, and barriers, and above all, doing it with the perfect hope that we can love and be loved unconditionally.

> **We need to learn how to make sacrifices and exceptions to keep our relationships balanced. The perfect blend of yin and yang, ups and downs, rights and wrongs, bridges, boundaries, and barriers, and above all, doing it with the perfect hope that we can love and be loved unconditionally.**

Lesson Nine

Celestial Fire

Purpose: Moon ceremonies have been a cleansing ritual for me throughout the years. During the next full moon, I ask you to conduct one of your own. Invite a few friends over, cook some good food, and light a bonfire. This is an activity that will bring in divine synchronicities.

Implementing the Law of Attraction with the release of any energy in your life that does not bring you happiness and joy, and manifesting into your life all the dreams, goals, and visions of your perfect future.

Tools:
- Paper (I recommend flying wish paper)
- Pen
- Candle wax
- Fire, friends, and food

Activity: Experience a moon ceremony.

step one:
Take two pieces of paper. On the top of one piece, write RELEASE and on top of the other write ATTRACTION.

step two:
Begin to write out everything you want to release and attract on each paper. Fold them up, seal them with candle wax, and toss them into the fire.

step three:
Watch the flames burn your release and attraction. Through this ritual, the Universe will free you of your worries and fears. Out with the old, in with the new.

$\textcircled{9}$

Our Emotions

Human beings are the sum of our emotions. Manifesting the emotions I want each day can be very difficult during times of trouble. The lessons and practices learned throughout my life, and shared within this book, are the hopeful knowing that life is truly what we make it. There are days when I wake up crying, two minutes later I'm laughing because I was crying, five minutes after that I'm pissed because I find dog pee on the floor. And these highs and lows of emotion all come before I can hear my chickens clucking outside my window.

This day has begun, and I'm already emotionally drained. During the troubled seas is when I take time to breathe, meditate, and collect my emotions. I try to figure out why I am feeling this way. It is almost always about another person and love. Something or someone connected to my love and care about them was the catalyst of why or how my emotions were reacting to the disconnection. You're lying to yourself if you have never experienced this.

> **"Wake at dawn with a winged heart and give thanks for another day of loving."—Khalil Gibran**

I have always been fascinated by the history of what, who, or where things come from. I have learned that the word *love* has so many definitions; there is no other word like it. The Greeks developed several definitions of love. *Eros* is romantic love. *Storage* is the love that we feel for family members. Oh, and that new puppy of mine who thinks my carpet is grass, her name is Love, too—add that to the list of definitions.

As a coach, the most important definition love is *phileo*, or comradeship. It is the type of love that is most important for teams. It is the love we feel for our teammates—the most basic feeling of goodwill for one another, a care for their health

"Wake at dawn with
a winged heart

&

give thanks
for another day
of loving."

—Kahlil Gibran

and well-being. I have taught that if team members love each other, they trust each other, they open to one another, they do not hold back with one another, they are unafraid to air their feelings, and they admit their mistakes, weaknesses, and concerns without fear of reprisal.

In immature relationships when we get our feelings hurt, we then choose to shut people out who care about us and want to help us. After this, for some reason we disconnect and put up barriers and block something out that we wanted all along. What are the boundaries? Why did we put up those barriers or boundaries in the first place instead of being open to everyone? Why can't we just be free to flow between each other?

Instead we become possessive. We try to have ownership and thoughts of how it should be, what is right, what is wrong, what we can or can't do. We put up those boundaries and say it's for our safety, but I do believe that many of the relationships end because of us, not the other person.

There is a difference between bridges, boundaries, and barriers. Bridges of course connect us with the people, places, and things we want to be a part of. Boundaries are used to create safe spaces for those same things to grow alongside us, but with some understanding that they don't get to just choose how they treat us. Barriers are meant to shut it all out completely, and though barriers may offer protection, sometimes they are disconnectors, which can be dangerous to our own well-being.

Learning how to orchestrate the different elements we want to use between these three things is tricky, but it is needed to have balance. It is even more difficult to try and figure out whether to build a bridge, boundary, or barrier just so we can coexist in a relationship that works well enough with the people in our lives.

It is much easier to blame boundaries and to disconnect then it is to look inside and ask ourselves: *What is causing me to break the relationship? What brought us together in the first place?* It is important that in times of relationship hardship, we consider how often we say that the relationship ended because of what the other person did to us. When there is enough trust and love between people, we can say something with real honesty and intent. We can create bridges and build friendships that are strong and beautiful. If we don't love and trust one another, then we aren't going to engage in open, constructive, and ideological conflict. In these situations, it is important to ask ourselves:

How do I get from this side to that side?

To be human and relatable is so powerful and allows connections between souls who are all experiencing pain or suffering. We're talking about the emotional connections we all really want, which is love. But it starts with us, and as we get more healthy with ourselves, we are wrestling with our own demons. At the end of the day, it's about self-worth, value, and knowing what you want or what you can give. Again, it's all about balance.

We are constantly asking ourselves: *What's wrong with me?* Really, we should just continue on our path until we attract what is meant for us. If my true self is love, then I have no problem loving lots of people. It is within this quest for love that we invite the souls who were meant to be our companions, lovers, and best friends. Time and time again I have asked, "God, is there any way I can have three lifetimes in the last stretch of my physical being? There are a lot of things that were missed in these fifty-five years of life because of my pride and ego. Now, here, I release my will and surrender to You." I hope you can do the same. Create beauty in our lives through hardships and understand that the people who hurt us are the people who we were meant to learn from. Rebuild based on what they planted in our gardens or along our paths, whether it was weeds or flowers.

There are people in our lives whom, for whatever reason, we don't get to or we don't want to sever relationships with because of how deeply rooted they are in our journeys. But, we do have the right to build bridges, boundaries, and barriers. It is our choice to decide how we want to create our gardens and fulfill our dream boards of *who we are* and *who we want to become.*

> **"It is necessary, and even vital, to set standards for your life and the people you allow in it."—Mandy Hale**

You and I have done this with our lovers, family members, and friends. Sometimes we choose to stay and fight and try and work it out. Sometimes it works, and sometimes it breaks. We have done this for years while building experiences. Rather than taking what we learn from each of these moments, sometimes we cast them away altogether. But why cast them away? They are a part of us. They will always be a part of us.

We can't forget that time of loving that you gave to them, you also gave to yourself. To try and deny that is to deny yourself some of life's greatest moments, and to do that means you are burying some of the most amazing moments of your life. Today, choose to say, "I am going to rejoice in the best moments that I can remember,

"Emotions are the
language of the soul."

—Karla McLaren

because those are the moments I am going to create millions of times again." Know these moments better and understand why we let fear keep those emotions away. However, sometimes we must pull away and regroup to create peace. We're always talking about boundaries and disconnection, but if we were to strip down everything and rely on each other, we would likely solve the origin of the terrible human behavior that we hurt each other with. At the right time, we can reconnect to the experiences and feelings we experienced to review what we learned from the past.

When you have an emotion that says *this feels out of place*, then it has to be talked about right then—whether it is with a friend or lover. Talk about how you are feeling, with yourself, with your person. Say, "I don't know if this is from abandonment, shame, or fear, but I need to talk through it so that you know where I have a scar that might need a little healing." We must learn to be aware enough to not engage in fight-or-flight, not protect, not run, not attack, not project anger, but instead realize your feelings and share the following sentiment: "I am having an experience, and it was painful for a minute. Something you said or did caused some chaotic ripple along the way. It's not about you, but can you talk through this with me, so you know me better?"

There have been many times that I needed to say something I was feeling, and I didn't. We can all relate. When we really care about someone dear to us, this is when we should be the most vulnerable and the most open with ourselves and them. It is always better to communicate emotions rather than bottling it all up inside, until one day it's too late. We must all be brave enough to say, "Something I am sensing isn't right; let's talk about it right there, right now."

When we don't get in our hearts to find out what the hell we did with our emotions and let all of our feelings come out, we bury alive everything of our past because it is too painful. This work is hard shit. It's beyond terrifying to go into our beings and try to figure out how we can balance ourselves again.

To learn how to love someone mentally, physically, and emotionally is the ultimate goal. Dive all in, or don't dive at all. When we put the ego, expectation, guilt, or responsibility on someone else, that is the beginning of putting up the first block to build a wall. Building a fortress to protect ourselves is only going to create more

heartaches in the end. Reveal every piece of you, and let the pieces fall where they may. The right one will come along and accept every part of you and your journey.

I want us to promise ourselves to have courage. Promise ourselves we will go into the emotional parts of our gardens, peaks, and valleys that we need to replant and take care of. We need to weed out the bad things and plant beauty along the way. When we don't do this, we are killing off our own peace, and poisoning all the beautiful plants woven throughout our path. Uproot the emotions and feelings that hurt so they don't come back to haunt us. Emotions buried alive never die. It doesn't need to be like this. It is a very small weed, and if you'll just take care of it, it will heal you, and your heart will be stronger.

Lesson Ten
The Joy Jar

Purpose: Creating gratitude day by day to capture all things amazing.

Tools:

- Mason jar, vase, or cookie jar
- Decorations (glitter, ribbon, crystals, etc.)
- Slips of paper
- Pen

Activity: Create a joy jar to collect moments of joy and look back on them to reconnect with yourself.

step one:

Select a jar that you want to decorate. I suggest taking a pottery class with some friends and designing your own joy jar. You can even take some old mason jars and decorate them with glitter, ribbon, or crystals. Write the words *JOY JAR* front and center on your masterpiece. This will be your constant reminder to record all the abundantly amazing life experiences of gratitude and joy.

step two:

Each day, take a slip of paper and write the date and good things that have happened that day. Fold up the paper and put it into the jar. Then on New Year's Eve or New Year's Day, sit down and go through the slips of joy written throughout the year.

(10)

Our Self-Love

While growing up, I loved going on adventures to discover new paths or places hidden within the red rocks of Moab, Utah. The treasures I would find were magnificent. From fossils to polished stones, the beauty of our world and its history was etched in the memory of the grounds my horse and I would trot on. Above all, my most favorite form of treasures to discover were crystals—sparkling, glittering pieces of Earth that mirrored light within the specks of each one found.

It's funny—as I look back on those adventures, I realize that our lives are just like the ones that roamed the Earth before us. The lives of people and creatures that now press into formations, marking their existence in time. These crystals that I found while growing up in such rich terrain are often like the emotional lessons we come across in our journeys. Sometimes they're not seeds, but rather they're treasures we pick up along the way, etching our existence too.

> **If I could offer you just one crystal of wisdom, it is this: if it was ever love in the beginning, it is always love.**

Heartaches, breakups, and disappointments are all experiences that seek to destroy our happiness. But all those shattered pieces pressed together form the crystals of wisdom we need. The most important lesson we could learn is that the love we seek to give to others will never work if we do not give that love to ourselves first. When we love unconditionally, we do not have to shift into a space of judgment or criticism of people because our self-love, or the lack thereof, is the mirror of our disconnections.

Source shows us true love in the following ways: Love is free, limitless, all-knowing, perfect, and cannot make a mistake. Pure love is incapable of failure and fear.

Without love of ourselves, we cannot create the wide open spaces that allow complete vulnerable connection with another soul.

Take all the broken pieces inside of you that need to be picked up and say to yourself, *You know what, I got you.* Because if you are not taking care of you, you suffocate your partners. Me giving everything into my life partner, and not letting myself have equal love too, wasn't about her. It was about my own lack of self-acceptance. Oftentimes in relationships, we make agreements that do not align with our true and authentic selves. I was doing this in previous relationships. I was shunning parts of me that were in fact, me, and not loving and accepting who I really was.

As life required me to start living alone again, digging around my garden became imperative. After taking off the layers, masks, and barriers, the light began to shine through. Self-discovery and self-love began to emerge and grow again. I was becoming clear on my personal passion and purpose that would lead back to wholeheartedness. It's taking the time to learn about who you are and who you want to become that's important, not only for others, but for yourself.

Does it matter if they love me back? No. Why not? Because *I love me.* I've gained the power and strength to pick up the parts and move forward with grace. Self-love requires pure strength, patience, and understanding of ourselves. When we learn to truly love ourselves, we create a synchronistic vibration that attracts what we send out into the Universe. Rather than spending all our time on social media, dating apps, and everything in between, we need to strive to become all the things we want, and Source will bring what has always been meant for us.

I am not saying it is easy. I have bawled ten thousand buckets of tears, but in every tear I ask, *Who is sad? Who do I not have? What part of me have I not loved enough that is feeling broken and abandoned?* As I have moved through my journey, I understand that a lot of it comes from the first seeds that were planted in my garden. The seeds of doubt, shame, fear, betrayal, and abandonment because I wasn't accepting of myself and my sexuality.

Every time I look at my dream board and I see the image of two brides and the saying of, "It's okay to be gay," it gives me a stressful feeling. That is that little self-sabotage that is holding the angels back from sending the love of my life. When we embark on the soul's journey of self-love, we learn that when we are not truthful with ourselves and the people we love, we violate the teachings of Don Miguel Ruiz's four agreements. We violate our truths.

What I need to be feeling and saying to myself is, *I'm gay today, and I'm proud of it.* I love me, and it's taken a hell of a long time to get here. I've created a lot of heartache for myself. I busted my ass because I didn't find a mentor to say, "Look at you, not them. You are not the victim. You are so powerful. You are a creator." The toughest people in the world are the greatest creators. They are the ones who know self-love is the most beautiful crystal of wisdom anyone could discover along their way.

I am seeking the people for my life who can say I love you freely, easily, and unconditionally. I too want everyone I love, in all the categories of love, to know I love them too. It's okay to go get what you want, but don't give with expectations of something being returned. Giving with expectation is not giving. My grandma used to say, "Never give something away that you want back. If you do, the relationship will be compromised." If you want to keep it, don't give it away. Both my grandparents and father lived during the Great Depression, they learned what it was to go without. It was a time of sharing, trading, and working together for the good of the community. There was not a need to steal, as their generation would give it to you. They taught the belief of, "If you steal my coat, take my shirt too." There is nothing that we are to covet, for God is the giver of all things. What is meant for us to have and to love will come in its own time and in its own way.

My God, my Source, always says, "There is nothing that your heart desires that I will not fulfill for your gratitude." I find that I am constantly wrestling with God's promise to us that we can receive anything that is worthy, so long as it is according to our purpose on Earth. Everything that we create in this life will be manifested or better via Source.

I really believe that when I wrestle with the questions and doubts that I have, I'm always too busy and frustrated to request: "Source, speak to me." In all my years of life, I have not yet created a partner who spiritually has the desire to match my faith. There have been glimpses of what my life may be like, and I just have to have the courage to pursue it with the patience to understand that none of it is on my time. It is all on God and Source's time.

We all need to get over our pride and ego and get on the path of love—love for others, but most importantly, love for ourselves. We've got to know and believe that we are the bomb dot com, that the world is our mountain, peaks, valleys, and canyons, and we are the crystals—the beautiful markings of our existence. There is someone that God wants for us, who meets all the laws that we want for ourselves. Someone who we can look at and say, "The core of me matches the core of you."

I believe that Source is going to hold off whatever is meant for us until we get done with our own purposes. So we should get it done. We need to get on the other side of all of this. We need to get through the highs and lows of our hearts.

"Live in the present. Do the things that need to be done. Do all the good you can each day. The future will unfold."

—Peace Pilgrim

When was the last time you did something you enjoyed?

At the end of the day, I want one thing and one thing only: to be tied to God and love, and to be loved on Earth like God loves me in Heaven. I am looking for that person, and guess who she is? She's right here.

Me, I am enough. You, you are enough.

We were looking for everyone else to fill that void, but the bottom line is the only one who can meet that expectation without frustration is yourself. When people don't meet us with what we want, we get frustrated. We get discouraged.

We have to decide who we want to be. Do we want to be the messy garden that stretches out with weeds along our path? Or do we want to be rooted in who we truly are, and grow to become who we were meant to be? We have the power to choose.

We need to commit to ourselves before we commit to others. To love yourself is to stand in who you are and whom you have come here to be. The true meaning of self-love and self-care will lead you to discovering a deeper truth of who you are, because the most supreme essence in the Universe is love; it is our purest guide. Without it, we have nothing and no direction. It is the Source of our happiness, and I can only imagine what healing and harmony we will bring to our Earth if we can all learn to love a little more each day, and above all, love who we are in this moment and in every moment to come.

So, now that we've gotten back up through the canyon, across a bridge, and encountered a block in our pathway, where to next? Where does the compass of love lead us? Who knows . . . because love has no rules, no regulations. Love does not know when to start or stop. It simply comes into our hearts and says,

> **"You and I can work together to learn how to be in unison, how to argue, how to agree to disagree, how to tell our truth, stand in our personal power, create with other souls, and love harder when it gets difficult."**

Love is our ultimate guide throughout this adventure. It is our compass.

Lesson Eleven

Mindful Mantras

Purpose: The greatest gift of self-love we can give is a basic mantra of repeating, "I am here for *you*." Buddhism teaches all types of mantras, which are words repeated over and over again to create a sense of oneness within ourselves. One of my greatest mantras has been the lesson of *The Four Agreements* written by Don Miguel Ruiz. Repeat after me:

I will live, breath, and speak my real truth.
I will not take anything personal.
I will make no assumptions.
I will demand my excellence and be the best I can be.

Tools:
- A quiet place to be still

Activity: In this activity, I want to add my own twist to his beautiful mantras.

step one:
Instead of saying "I will . . ." I want you to begin each mantra with "I am . . ." For the next five minutes, take a moment to visualize yourself watching ocean waves. On each wave that comes to shore say "I am," and as the wave goes out, say "my true self."

step two:
Recite the second agreement. Say "I am whole, and nothing is personal. I am perfect, and nothing is personal." Continue with, "I am free of making assumptions."

step three:
Finally, say the words, "I am demanding my excellence and the best I can be."

Part Three

For Our Minds

Our Oceans

The truest parts of who we are lay within the depths of our minds. If you think about it, to cross any ocean would be a vast and dangerous journey, especially the ocean that flows in our heads. However, the end destination is always worth it. As we enter part three of *Our Soul's Journey*, I want you to imagine yourself emerging from the mountain, peaks, and valleys of your heart. Your pathway begins to transform from rocks and dirt to a sea of sand. To understand the deepest parts of who we are, we now begin to embark on the journey through our oceans of thoughts, memories, dreams, and mindsets.

Chapters

Our Thoughts

They say that everything leads back to the ocean. After every rainstorm in Hawaii, the shorelines are dotted with debris from the mountain. The waterfalls that stream back out to sea carry broken branches, leaves, dirt, bottles, and wrappers . . . the list could go on and on about the things you would find the morning after rain and wind.

I mention Hawaii specifically because a former volleyball player of mine grew up on the North Shore of Oahu. On a hometown visit one summer, she found herself in the ocean, surrounded by flakes of dead leaves, plastic bottles, and branches from the drainage that bled back into the water after a storm. As we spoke of her trip, she continued telling me her story, and she said that in that moment, she had two choices: return back to the beach or to swim further out into the ocean to escape the layer of debris that floated around her.

I asked her what choice she made and laughed when she answered me. "I swam out of course. Never mind that it was more dangerous."

Now that I think about it, yes, it was riskier for her to swim farther out. The water

is deeper, the currents are stronger, and we're all aware of the creatures that live below the surface in the deep sea. I was delighted with her response. Knowing her and knowing how similar our personalities and mindsets are, this is what makes this story relevant to my own. With every word she spoke, I envisioned how her experience

often relates to all of us. How many times have we begun to embark on our journey through our minds, to understand ourselves better, but instead of pushing through debris, we choose to return back to the shore.

As we grow beyond the seeds of our life's garden and journey through our mountains and valleys, we then walk through the beach and sand to enter our oceans. Oftentimes we find the debris of negative thoughts, experiences, memories, and more floating around us as we set to cross the depths of our minds. The depths of who we are. We must only have courage and faith to know that from the beginning of our existence, to the end, Source is with us.

From the moment we are born, we have a subconscious. We don't exist, and then we do. We come with a natural brilliance of being, and from the minute we take that first breath, and the heart begins to beat, our existence becomes real. We are pure, whole, perfect, and have a glowing essence of thoughts just waiting to be created. I have always believed that "thoughts become things."

There are so many questions we could sift through: What is the mind? What is thinking? What is learning?

When we begin to look at what we learn subconsciously in our environments, we realize that our thoughts truly are already here, waiting to exist in the Universe. We are our thoughts. Just as the Roman Emperor Marcus Aurelius once said, "Our life is what our thoughts make it."

| "Thoughts Become Things."

To put it simply, we all have the power within our minds to change our world and the world of others. There's an ocean of thoughts in our heads. Think about a time when you were just sitting and pondering when all of a sudden you have a thought. It pops in and out, and you're left wondering, *Well, where did that come from?* The one thing that I am certain of is that thoughts and energy are synchronistic, and where there is energy, there is power. The trick is learning how to create these powerful thoughts that then become tangible and real.

It is estimated that each day we sort through roughly 60,000 thoughts. The depth of a person's mind can be as deep as an ocean or as shallow as a wave crashing on the shore. I guess you could say it takes the brave ones to swim out into the vast sea of thoughts in search of meaning and understanding of what and who we are and why we are here.

When we are born, we're perfect, whole, and complete. We have no limits, no lacks, no labels. Then one day, we're a little kid who makes a mistake, and the reactions to that mistake cause us to take on limiting beliefs and identities. We carry these with us. As we walk our path throughout life, we absorb information in the environments that we go through, whether it's from people, places, or experiences. It doesn't even matter whether you grow up in Moab, Utah, or London, England... at the end of the day, we are all humans living and learning from what we see, hear, or feel. Our ocean of thoughts flows every moment we are alive, because as we gather information, we store it, and from time to time, our thoughts resurface when we come across a specific sight, taste, smell, or sound. It all comes rushing forward to trigger our minds and thoughts.

Growing up, I wanted to wear cowboy boots and Levi's. I didn't want to wear dresses, and I damn sure did not want to wear high heels. This is where I gained my first label of, "tomboy" or "stud." First, I was not a boy, and second, I was not a male horse set aside for breeding. How little we think about the connotation of our words. Even when I began to invest my time in athletics, I was considered a jock because I loved to play sports.

I began to battle within my own mind what was right or wrong, and why couldn't I have, be, and do what I loved without the limiting labels. I learned the most about limits, lack, and labels during my coming to a realization that I was attracted to girls.

> ## We don't really understand what limit, lack and labels mean to us, until we begin to suffer from abandonment, betrayal, shame, or all of the above.

It's like subtle poison being released into our gardens that spreads throughout our path, eventually washing out into our ocean, creating another form of debris.

We don't always notice that based on the painful or uncomfortable things we go through, we begin to take on the words like a poison to our abundance. We take on these labels thrown at us, and it becomes a part of our masks that we wear. From the moment we are born, to the moment we encounter our first experience of shame, guilt, fear, or abandonment, our thoughts are the only thing that keep us from becoming what others say or do to try and destroy the life we are capable of creating. This is the garden we have the power to grow.

We can *have, be,* or *do* anything in life if we all work with our Source of infinite power. Natural laws of the Universe will attract what we mentally project. Images in our

"Willing to experience aloneness, I discover connection everywhere; turning to face my fear, I meet the warrior who lives within."

—Jennifer Welwood

What moments in your childhood made you who you are today?

mind of what we are thinking will come to life. The Law of Attraction is obedient and will always respond to our thoughts. The mind creates what is perceived, and a positive thought is one hundred times more powerful than a negative thought.

If our lives are what our thoughts make, then my question for all of us is why do we sometimes try to go off path of what we think or feel is right for our own well-being? We're all trying to swim against the current instead of gently going with the natural flow of knowledge that everything happens the way it was supposed to happen. I've been trying to get into the habit of asking myself: *How does this moment feel?* When I have an off-course thought, this process of taking a second to slow down and feel the moment I am in has helped me to catch those thoughts when I'm fighting against the natural current. It helps keep me on my path.

In our human mind, most of us aren't always so adept at catching the off-course thoughts. When we don't catch them, change them, and get back on our path to purpose, we continue to create what we think, which produces a negative karma flow. *What we know, we create . . . what we think, we become.* This needs to be a daily mantra and positive affirmation that is said both out loud and echoed internally.

In sports training, imagery is everything. In volleyball, I've always taught that when the mind stops to think, the body waits. The average time for a rally in women's volleyball is eight seconds, and let me tell you, a whole lot of shit could happen in eight seconds. The moment the whistle blows, someone serves over the net, a player passes the ball to the setter, the setter sets it to the hitter, and the hitter does one of many things: kills the ball, resulting in an instant point; hits into the net or blocker's hands; hits it out; or doesn't hit it at all because she decides to tip, roll shot, or simply gets the ball over. Now this is just a few scenarios of hundreds of different plays that could happen in the game, my point is, there are only about eight seconds for six girls to each step up and do their part to make sure they get the point.

I mention this scenario because if a player has to think in depth about what to do in an instant as a fifty-mile-per-hour ball is being hit toward their face, the play would already be over by the time that athlete had a chance to even think. So, we teach in volleyball that it needs to become a subconscious and automatic response. It has to be a natural brilliance to know that in that moment, they must either put their hands up to deflect the ball, resulting in a dig and an opportunity for their teammates to score a point against their opponent, or a bloody nose and check out of the game. Life is just like this. Sometimes we get time-outs to think and create a plan, and sometimes we get fifty-mile-per-hour balls spiked toward our face. How we choose to battle is the greatest choice of all. That's why everything we do needs practice. It needs to be halting the off-course thought.

"You must be
100 percent
committed to each action.

If you have any doubts,
your body will not know what to do.

Let your routines switch you
from the thinking mode
to the trusting mode."

—*Mind Gym*

Stop, rethink, refocus. Get a game plan together, get back up, get back out there and battle till the end.

This book was created to teach people how to coach themselves back to empowerment. We need to be able to go from beginner to intermediate to collegiate to professional in this game of life. Along the way, those who really want to be awakened journeyers will merge paths with those who have the same end goal in mind. These people become our teammates, the souls that we get to bond and battle with.

In coaching, we teach kids to dream big and go for it. At some point in time, dreaming big becomes pressure, and then fear, lack, and limit overtake our thoughts. It's scary to chase what we think to be true, or what we envision for ourselves, but it is so necessary because our failures often become our greatest lessons.

Every day we wake up, we get twenty-four hours to better ourselves and our world. Rather than spending 60,000 thoughts that circulate in our minds on things not worth putting energy to, we get to swim past the debris and dive deep into our ocean of thoughts. Oftentimes, we will find the lessons and beautiful moments meant for us, even in the vast blue waves. Just as we discover crystals laced in our mountains and valleys, we will also find the pearls of wisdom waiting to be collected and carried throughout the rest of our journey.

We must strive to not go off course with all of our mental time, creating a current of negative thoughts. Match the positive energy with positive thoughts to blossom into the best version of yourself. Become a master and professional, like a Buddhist or a monk—a person so in sync with their thoughts that everything just flows to them.

The amazing truth is that our thoughts will become things. They become real moments and memories, pearls that you will keep and place along your path. I'm coaching you right now, asking you to pour all your mental energy into thinking big and praying big. This takes great faith and focused power to create the things we will manifest. Dare to do the unimaginable.

Here's to pushing past the debris, flowing with the current, and focusing on the next eight seconds of our lives, when we get to think about this moment, this play.

"There is no passion
to be found
playing small,
in settling for a life
that is less than
the one
you are capable
of living."

—Nelson Mandela

Lesson Twelve
Restoring Peace to Our Chaotic Thoughts

Purpose: As Buddha taught, we are joy, but we are also pain; we are love and also ignorance. It is not a battle between the two. When you are angry that is one energy; mindfulness is the other energy.

Tools:
- A quiet space to breathe

Activity: The object of this practice is to experience the love you have for yourself and others. This lesson won't make a ton of sense if you have not seen the movie *Inside Out*. (I highly recommend if you have a free night, watch it.)

step one:
Take a moment and observe the emotions you're feeling currently. Imagine that every one of your emotions is a character. Visualize joy and anger sitting with you. Imagine as if you are the mother or father of pure love.

step two:
Talk with each emotion as you would a small child until they come together as one. Question what caused the emotion to surface. Obviously, you can't just punish anger for being what it is, but you can address the feeling and the moment that is associated with that emotion. Instead of letting these feelings control you, make a conscious effort to control your thoughts that control your feelings. This lesson will transform negative energies into joy and peace.

Any time you're feeling overwhelmed or unsure of your emotions or their origins, return to this visualization exercise. Never shame yourself for feeling an emotion in a given moment; emotions are simply messengers asking us to pay attention to how we're feeling.

"The greatest battle we face as human beings is the battle to protect our true selves from the self the world wants us to become."

—e e cummings

(12)

Our Manifestations

My dream board is layered with pictures of who I am and who I want to be. While our hearts are the compass, we use to guide us, our dream boards are like the visual maps we use to cross the ocean of our minds. Every morning, I wake up to my dream board sitting on my dresser; it reflects the memories that I have lived and the moments I plan to create.

At this point in our journey through this book, it is a good time to see if there is anything we should either add or replace on our dream boards, because we know that thoughts evoking great emotion will manifest quickly. We want to manifest things we *really* want, so we should be careful what we're constantly visualizing and imagining for ourselves.

When we want things to happen in our life, we need to manifest it to be here. That is what creating our best life is. It's not about just hoping for your dreams without acting on them. We've all got to go get what we want in life. I teach all my athletes to make a habit of making their bed every day. Why? This completion of one goal leads to an energy vibration that sets in motion accomplishment and inspired action toward dreams and goals.

If you were to ask me what I want most in life right now, my answer is to be aligned emotionally, physically, spiritually, and mentally. If we go through this process each day of body, heart, mind, and soul, we can manifest anything into our lives.

I've always believed that I must follow the passion of my life to make results happen. I'm a visionary. I see an idea that feels purposeful and fun, then create it into reality. I've asked myself many times, *Is this purpose or is this ego?* If manifesting is saying that it already is, then act like it already is. Just do it, go for it, and don't hold back.

"In the end, only three things matter:
how much you loved,
how gently you lived,
& how gracefully
you let go of things
not meant for you."

—Buddha

Is your ocean flowing with positive affirmations and manifestations?

Trust the one who makes it all possible, whether it is God, Universe, Energy, or Cosmos. The natural knowing that everything is going to work out brings peace and joy back to life, and it releases the tension around your desires that is keeping them from coming into your reality. Live your best life . . . because you get to!

Manifestation is real and powerful, but so is trusting and believing. We know manifesting is clearing all the bad energy, ego, and mind out of the way to then attract the good things meant for us. When we're trying to sort through fear of what we want to happen and speak our beliefs out loud, sometimes our minds can't believe it, so we shorten the goal. Our own thoughts block the flow and attraction of our deepest desires, and they water down our biggest dreams out of fear.

A question for us to think about is, *What's the difference between expectation and manifestation?* The answer—it's nothing. When we believe what's really coming is meant for us, it comes in every moment that is made for us to encounter. This process doesn't need to be a two-hundred-year path of question and answer, because most of what came to me was when I was passionately pursuing my dream and my ideas. That's when it all manifested and became real. The dream board was just a visual representation of the things I wanted most in life. The outcome was the result of my Source's power to align my path and journey through every experience I have lived through.

I know my God loves me so much that when I fall completely in love with myself, He is going to bring in an equal match of love. Most of my control issues are because of my fear and power to put up the boundary of protection. Though sometimes I choose to walk off path, thinking I can do it all by myself, most times, I find myself lost and begin to manifest things that are negative and against my flow. I can just imagine God saying to me, "I have a lesson here if you would just calm down. I will work it out a whole different way—a way that is more amazing."

We've all got to learn to only focus on what we can control. Consistently strive to be in the space where if we're just controlling the next eight seconds, we can be aligned with our purpose and the moments we wish to manifest into our lives.

Energy and thoughts are synchronistic, and so is manifestation. As soon as the energy changes, and it doesn't feel good, the manifestation gets slower to reach us. If we listen to everybody else's energy, it can also turn off our energy because we get discouraged. Sometimes, we need to ignore the outside noise, and reflect internally to our heart and mind, and ask ourselves: *What do you want? How do you want it to look and feel?*

If you focus on what you want, you will attract what you want. If you focus on the lack of what you want, you will attract more of the lack. If you are paying attention to the way you are feeling, you will always know whether you are focused on positive or negative affirmations.

Be in your skin, right here, right now. When you feel like you're getting scattered everywhere—like the items that fell out of the bag—just pause, breathe, and focus. Manifestation is an instant rewrite to what feels good, what is said positively in our minds. It is how we speak to ourselves within ourselves. How can we get good enough to quickly manifest with our mind? How quickly can we get from one repetition of perfect to become nine out of ten or even ten out of ten?

In sports, there's no such thing as perfect. You've got to be disciplined to get good enough to play, and from there, you get to take what you're good at, find your opponent's weakness, and put your best up against their worst. It's all about tactics, and most times our opponents are ourselves. We are our greatest enemies, because we hold the power within our minds to limit ourselves from what we are all capable of. When we can mentally practice becoming our best selves, we then have the ability to defeat our own internal opponents. Life is a game, and sometimes we're blocking our own manifestations and playing ourselves.

With any task or process, once you become adept at the fundamentals and roll through them over and over again without error, you become great at whatever it is. Most of the time in athletics, kids won't push themselves at game speed to be a consistent eight out of ten times. They'll push themselves just enough to do what they want. Athletes work their ass off to be a starter, but it does not matter who starts... it's about who finishes.

I can't tell you the number of young women I've coached who started and had the potential to become the best, but they never even made it to the middle, far less to the finish. I want you and I to be the few who start and finish strong on this journey. Even when our manifestations, hopes, dreams, and prayers (which are all the same thing by the way) don't come to fruition. Life is a constant battle of ups and downs, good and bad, limits, lack, and labels, and it's always coming hard and fast. As souls on this journey throughout life, we get to manifest what we think and believe we deserve.

Day in and day out, we get to have the courage to not only hope for clearer and brighter moments, but to know that miracles do happen because manifestation is real. This I know to be true.

Question:

What mental debris is blocking your way today?

Lesson Thirteen
Manifest Your Life Forward

Purpose: This lesson is designed to guide you in writing your life backward. Begin with the end in mind. Every day, put all the high vibrations you can into feeling how your life is going to look and feel when your affirmations and manifestations come true.

Tools:
- Bath tub
- Sea salt
- Journal
- Pen

Activity: Take one of the areas of wellness and write your life backward.

step one:
Choose one of the following dimensions we discussed previously as the focus of this exercise: physical, emotional, occupational, intellectual, social, or spiritual.

step two:
Start by filling up your bath tub with hot water and adding bath salts. Cleanse your body and relax.

step three:
After the bath, pull out your journal and *dream big* in one of the dimensions of your life. Write it out as though you are living it at this very moment. What do you really, really want it to look like? After you have felt and lived your dream, write your answers to the following questions.

What is one step I can take today to make this manifestation come true?

On a separate piece of paper, write out the answers to these questions. When you are finished, perform a burning ceremony or bury them in a hole:

Ask your Source to reveal what mental block you might have in the way. Release that thought on a separate piece of paper.

Consider why you can't have this. Get all the blocks out of the way by writing these limiting beliefs down, clear your path, and believe.

Complete this exercise for any dimension in your life you'd like to see change in. You can also complete this exercise many times for the same dreams and goals, as each time you complete it, you'll step closer to bringing the details into reality.

(13)

Our Memories

I know we all have some memories we wish we could forget. However, given the choice, I still would choose to keep them all. These are the times that challenged us to the core of our being, the ones we call shattering, difficult, or hard. The ones we want to scrub from our memories. What would happen if we scrubbed them away? Then we also wipe out the amazing, fantastic times in life that make it all worthwhile. I am humbly grateful for my life; every valley and peak has given me so much. I've been young, and I hope my experience shows others how to do hard things along life's path to aging wisdom.

There are nights I lay awake pondering emotional times. These are times of grief, like losing my dad and gran who were my best friends. These are times of fear regarding disappointing my mom and significant people in my life. Being fired from my dream career. Betrayed by people whom I trusted with my businesses. Getting my heart broken over and over again. But the memories of my sexual assaults cannot be buried alive. Having the courage to speak up, speak out, and empower others to talk with those inner children who were violated and left hurting is so important. Giving voice to the children, that is the path to healing. Teaching them to be brave enough to tell their stories, write them, or speak them is the only way to release the poison from your life and body. Your life will thank you. It will not be easy, but it will be worth it.

When we carry around anger, hatred, or malice in our hearts and heads, we are carrying around poison inside us. It is unbelievably difficult to learn how to let go of the tragedies we have suffered through, but it is so critical to give up those pains. The poison of buried trauma manifests itself throughout our bodies. Disease, injury, muscle pains, and aches—you name it, the body shows it in so many different ways. Finding the courage to go into the memory of when I was sexually abused by an old man, a man whom my family thought could be trusted, has been my greatest life challenge. He changed an innocence in me that was precious, and a part of me

"Sometimes

the water

is calm, and

sometimes it is

overwhelming.

all we can do is

learn to swim."

—Vicki Harrison

was destroyed forever because of it. I sometimes think to myself, *Well, why didn't you just tell him to fuck off?* When I was five years old, I was weak and an easy target for abuse. As I got older, I carried around that shame and guilt of blaming myself for letting it happen. But I didn't let it happen. He stole it from me. And until this day, that memory, that moment haunts me and is something I am still learning to process these many years later.

It has been hell trying to heal from this, and it is all a part of my journey to empowerment. Seeking forgiveness of not only myself but for him as well has been the most strenuous path I have ever taken. And even writing about it right now feels icky and unsettling. I just want to shut it off, move on from the memory, and get off this limiting, lacking, and fearing thought. I am constantly in my own mind asking myself, *How do I bury it, turn it off, and not feel gross or shameful?* Because yes, there are some memories that we all wish we could forget, but we don't get to. To find the strength and bravery to dive deep and seek the meaning to understand that everything happens to us for a reason. No matter how painful. Our souls must go through these trials to mold us into who we were always meant to be.

The memory is us. It has made us who we are. There is no section in the book that says, "Take that bad memory, plant it far away from your path, and move on." We can't go out into our head and try and bury everything that hurts or haunts. We need to acknowledge it all.

> ## Out of sight, out of mind does not work because it can be out of sight, but still in our mind.

It's kind of like those dangerous creatures that lurk below the surface. The ones you risk to swim through to get to a clearer space of ocean. You can try to move, push, or bury the memory, but it will always be there. The lessons and pearls you will find are always hidden in the deeper parts of who we are. In each and every moment we suffer through, we will come to know why we flow through what we go through. Trusting your compass and map always requires the strength to forgive, heal, and clear the debris so you can swim in the beautiful sea called your best life.

As the oldest in my family, I've always felt this need to be the toughest, the most mature, the one who always says, "I got this." If you're the oldest, you know the feeling of wanting to hold it all together. God forbid, when shit happens, the eldest put all their emotions aside to handle the task. The consequences I have had to pay have been dear, because now, as I write this book, everything that I did not heal from is beginning to resurface. The wounds from those painful memories did not mend right, creating scars that are messy and rough.

When we try to block out the memory and the pain, it catches up to us because we didn't really want to face it. It's okay to feel though it. When my dad died, I remember I held it together for as long as I could until I got into the car after his funeral . . . then it all released. I was sobbing so hard that I couldn't even see while driving. I had to pull over and collect myself. I didn't think about it then, but I realize now that there were so many people that could've helped me through that. Instead, I tricked myself into thinking I was so strong that I didn't need any help. But when I was finally alone, I let it go and it nearly drowned me. I didn't want anyone to see me breaking, and it made everyone think I had no emotion. It's taken me years to learn that there is nothing wrong with being vulnerable and revealing how we truly feel. It is so vital to take those steps to unveil the masks we try to portray to the world.

What happens in our minds is that the ocean of thoughts, dreams, and memories is in a constant flow, but as humans we try to suppress the fear of loss, pain, anger, and hurt. We try to hold it in and push it back, much like how the ocean draws back as it begins to build up its wall of water. And then all of a sudden everything at the back end of the memory slams to the front of the mind, creating a force so strong that the ocean of things we struggled to push back gets thrusted forward by the currents of reality, orchestrating a tsunami of destruction within our heads. For me, my initial reaction has always been to shut off my emotion and not feel any of it as the tsunami tears through my insides, destroying everything in its path and my life's garden.

The fear of not having courage and not dealing with the memories that haunt us will always create more pain. When we confront these things, the wounds do heal and the scars that are created are strong. This strength shows the world who we are and what we can do with the faith in Source and infinite possibility.

This is the mental toughness we all want to learn. Taking away the negative energy that matches with the memories we suffer through is taking away the power of those negative and bad thoughts, feelings, and memories. Go into these memories and find your high vibration so that you are not in addiction, disconnection, or judgement of ourselves and of others.

Grow through the memory, and understand it rather than deny it. Most of us will try to suppress the memory because we think we can't deal with it and it's more than we can handle. But we are stronger than we let ourselves believe. No one can walk through our journey for us. We have to do that. If we don't embark on our path of good, bad, and everything in between, we won't have the strength needed for the next wave of trial and tribulation. There are moments, days, and years in our lives when the tsunami, typhoon of storms, rains, and every other version of hell come pouring down on us. There are spaces we end up in where we have no due north, no direction, no idea what is going on, and many people will take their life through it.

What memory do you need to let flow in and out of your life?

The movement from hell to peace in the mind is challenging, so how do we get there? Creating time to write, meditate, and breathe is wonderful wound therapy. These activities and many more assist us with healing trauma. Knowing that we all deserve to be free of post-traumatic stressors and that many people have the skills to guide us through these barriers is awesome news.

I do not need to be shameful because bad things happen to good people, and it doesn't need to make people's insides torn. Our memory patterns are what shapes us into who we are now. Deal with the memory and issues, acknowledge them, and thank them for bringing the lesson that you were meant to learn from. We don't have to carry the poison with us, and we don't have to let it spread throughout our pathway. We can let the flow of life happen to us without building up tsunamis of destruction within our heads.

Let it go; let it flow.

Lesson Fourteen

Breathe & Build Your Rock Altar

Purpose: This lesson allows you to get connected with nature. It will allow the space needed to align with your life's pain, passions, and purpose. Giving everything daily to your meditation altar will allow the energies inside to flow.

Tools:

- Rocks

- Sticks

- Leaves

- Seashells

- Feathers

- Crystals

- Any natural element that is calling to you

Activity: Create a spiritual rock altar where you can physically go daily in your home and reconnect with your Source, self, and soul.

step one:
Take a hike along a stream, mountain path, or other areas where you can find a beautiful rocks and other natural materials.

step two:
Collect rocks, sticks, leaves, anything that is calling to you. When you pick an item up, if it feels like it is drawing into your heart, keep it, if it feels heavy, leave it. Focus your attention on looking for specific items that are calling you to design your nature artwork.

step three:
Take these items home and make yourself a natural rock altar where you can go and offer up to God or your Source all the personal intentions you have for the day. Each day, visit your altar and speak of gratitude, love, and desired manifestations you want to create, while also releasing pain and emotional blocks. Incorporate this practice with daily meditation or breathing exercises.

(14)

Our Mindsets

How do we push ourselves to those uncomfortable places and mindsets where we grow the most? As a coach, you teach athletes how to stretch and build a consistent regimen for themselves. It all begins with how we start our day. When we wake up in the morning, we've got to learn to say, "This is the best day of my life," because we create what we think about. So, get up, make your bed, and read your sticky note gratitude notes and "I love you" statements off the mirror while brushing your teeth. Do something for yourself and give gratitude to someone else. Consciously unclutter your life, get rid of all that stuff lying around, and have a place for everything.

One thing you will find is that this simple act will not only clean up your spaces, but it will reduce stress and save time. A lot of people push Snooze on their alarm. Instead of pressing Snooze, use that extra ten minutes to write in your journal. Describe what you are going to manifest in the next twenty-four hours. Before you go to bed, look at how you did and smile over your success. If you didn't get something quite right, no worries, move it forward, for tomorrow is another day. Looking at our dream boards each night prior to sleeping helps us subconsciously create our destinies.

I think there's something to be said about the hour of power. The hour of power is when you select a task you want to complete and set your timer for sixty minutes. Each day, if we place complete focus on long-term projects using the hour of power technique, it will help to assure we accomplish the desired outcome. Go all-in for sixty minutes, no excuses. Concentrate and execute on the one thing you want the most for your life, and you'll rejoice in how many little things you accomplish each day.

Athletes know they must go to practice to get better at their sports. But oftentimes, we stop there. We don't continually practice day in and day out how to become the best versions of ourselves in every aspect, not just in one area. The whole goal of this journey is to become a master of our *Empowerment Journey*. Practice makes

Reflection:

———

What are you grateful for today?

THOUGHTS

BECOME

THINGS

greatness. To create habits that create our best life road map, we need to schedule our priorities around purpose and passion. Creating the plan begins with taking the first step. To create one new habit, anchor it to an existing habit. For example, while brushing your teeth recite your daily gratitude statements. If we know how to defeat our defeats, then we will become champions of our lives.

Negative flow is manifested with our thoughts and beliefs of lack and limit. These thoughts bring about a tidal wave of emotion, and we create a vicious cycle that feels deep, dark, and often so overwhelming. When I lost my dog Taylor, everything that I had already been through already made me feel like I was drowning. But it was my mindset to stay strong for myself that carried me through. It was my will power to push myself to that uncomfortable space where I have grown the most.

Reflecting on Taylor has been a joyous process for me. She was love. She represented unconditional love and unwavering commitment to all the opposites of betrayal, abandonment, and shame. She was pure and sweet. Having to choose to allow her to end the pain and suffering of cancer was the greatest love I have ever been asked to give—letting go of this love of my life so that she would not suffer any longer. I learned so much in those hours of loving her and giving her all her favorite treats in life. I consciously choose to focus on all the wonderful things of life she enjoyed: vanilla ice cream, eggs with cheese, and a tub of water to lay in during a hot July day.

I took all that emotion of loss and grief I was feeling and put it into action, words, and gratitude to serve her before she went with the angels. I want to live my life each day with the growth mindset of thinking, acting, and expecting goodness. See the negative emotion, look at the thought, and write the ending with a beautiful tribute to what you want next. Rewrite negative thoughts by putting action to them instead of not believing, not expecting, and not allowing. We have a human form and a spirit form that are always with us. When we are feeling bad, what can we do to change our energy? Stop, breathe, feel the moment, and begin to mentally picture how your aura can become enlightened. We can train our minds to focus on right here, right now, with gratitude and love. Stop the emotional thinking that sabotages us from our highest vibrations.

Creating a growth mindset is done by putting our thoughts on what we want now or soon. When we have a thought focused on the past that creates a negative emotion, we have backward thinking and are not in the flow with our life's journey. The problem we may all have is that even though we can be doing a lot of stuff, we are not doing all those things to our best, but rather just good enough to get by. We are tricking ourselves into thinking that we are swimming through our oceans, trying to get through it, but in reality, we remain stuck in areas of debris that have us going nowhere. It's probably one of the most dangerous moments on our journey. Yes, I could have just chosen to float around in debris of pain and loss when Taylor died, but I didn't. I sent her off with every piece of my heart and soul. With all losses there is gain. I believe all the loves of my life that have passed with death are now my guardian angels, guiding me along life's journey.

To have a fixed mindset that is only focused on past events and experiences is unhealthy and unsafe. If we remain trapped in our heads, we remain trapped in the middle of the ocean, the deepest and darkest parts. Learning to create the positive mindset that creates the greatest versions of ourselves is the bravest act of love we can give to our souls. It is that conscious effort to just keep swimming, while doing our best. That is what I call success.

Every so often, I run a simple test on my athletes. I tell them to get on the line and sprint from one side of the gym to the other and back. I blow the whistle, and off they go. I can see the ones who jog their way there, the ones who sprint just enough to look like they're trying, and the ones who don't even put half effort to get from one side to the other.

After the athletes complete this drill, I pull out a one-hundred-dollar bill. Crisp, green, and ready to be seen. I then tell the players to line up again. Only this time I explain to them that the first athlete who can run to the other side and back in under eleven seconds gets the bill. In this moment, you can see them gearing up to win. I blow the whistle, and off they go again. No one has ever crossed the line in under eleven seconds, but after they have each run through and completed the test, I tell them to gather around me. I then say one sentence to them: "Raise your hand if you put in the same amount of effort into running your fastest the first time when there was no reward, as you did the second time."

Never once in my thirty years of coaching has a single person raised their hand. I mention this story because this is often the mentality and mindset that we all have: let me do just enough to make it look like I am swimming my hardest or just enough to get through this current, to go from shore to shore. It's tricky to avoid thinking like this because we all do it. My grandmother used to teach me that when we don't do something well, we will never have satisfaction, and without satisfaction, we do not have pride.

To be able to live each and every day with the mindset of, "I am going to sprint or swim my fastest with or without a reward," is where exhilaration for living your best life comes. It's required because we get to wake up every morning with a full day ahead of us: Eight seconds of each moment that add up to twenty-four hours.

"Just keep swimming"

-Dory, *Finding Nemo*

Are you swimming hard enough?

Twenty-four glorious hours that we have to create, think, learn, play, laugh, love, and cry.

> **Never give the negative in life more time than it deserves. Life is our game, and each day we have to live and breathe our daily manifestations that lead to our life's destiny and dreams.**

Whatever the negative thoughts we have, we can change by putting in positive imagery and moving everything forward. Everything is an asking: *What do I want? How does it feel? How do I create a positive that I want?* In volleyball, I have my athletes do visualization training. This training is implemented by having the athlete watch high-level players executing various skills at the highest level of perfection. This training then allows the athlete to visualize themselves in the professional athlete's body executing the exact same skills, feeling each serve, pass, set, or hit as perfectly as the professional. Over and over and over again, we have each player visualize themselves perfecting the skill. Go through it, playing it in their minds, feeling each skill performed perfectly, because the mind does not know the difference between what is really or what is visualized. When the athlete begins playing the game, they now have a mental image of themselves perfectly executing each skill. If an error occurs, we have them immediately go back to their perfect mental image of themselves executing the skill. This provides a level of confidence, and the body will begin to focus on these next skills, rather than on the past mistake. The body will follow what the mind portrays to it. It is the entire concept of *thoughts become things.* All of it is imagery.

If each day, we can consistently get into a habit of thinking, writing, and speaking our truths and our goals, we will be able to manifest amazing moments into existence. Going back to our visual dream board to think and visualize every moment we seek to live from this day, and each day to follow, is the ultimate way to live and love our best lives.

We are our thoughts; we are our dreams. Learning to live in your truth is intimidating, but you and I are brave, and we can do this. I want us to dream about our dream lovers, careers, wishes, bucket lists, self-worth—all of it—and let it flow to us. We need to promise ourselves that every day Source wakes us up, we will have the mindset to think about the best life we want; manifest what feels good to our body, heart, mind, and soul; understand that every memory is just a part of who we were and who we will become; know that our greatest defeats will be our greatest lessons; and, above all, that our mindsets are not our limits, lacks, and labels.

Who we are in this moment, in this eight-second rally of play and every set of rallies to come, is gearing us up to become who we were meant to be. Every day, every play, every moment, is what we set our minds to think and believe.

Here and now, imagine the best version of yourself. Trust your compass. Trust your map. Complete the journey across your *Ocean of Thoughts, Memories, and Mindsets*, and create your best life.

Lesson Fifteen
Pen & Paper

Purpose: Journaling is an amazing way to organize your mind and clear your head space. It will raise your vibration by releasing worries onto the paper, freeing them from your ocean. The lesson is automatic writing. I want you to read each prompt out loud and begin writing as soon as you finish reading. This is a recording of everything that comes to mind—no editing, no spell checks, just writing. Another good way to do this activity is to speak into a recording app. (I highly recommend Otter.) Speak your mind, thoughts, manifestations, whatever it may be. Good luck!

Tools:
- Journal
- Pen

Activity: Make it a goal to write every day for at least ten to fifteen minutes.

Journal prompts:

- Create task lists to complete.
- Set goals for the week.
- Consider things you are grateful for, memories you love, or people you adore.
- Draft a wish list.
- Write about a time that was difficult, but you kept trying.
- Express gratitude and love for the new beginnings that life gives you.
- Create a bucket list.
- Finish this sentence: "I deserve love because..."
- Take this moment to appreciate the power of words and how lucky we are to be able to use them to communicate and express ourselves. What words would you like to share with yourself?
- Write about the success you have had because of your own efforts.
- Finish this sentence: "I love myself because..."
- Finish this sentence: "I made choices today that made me a better person because..."
- Express gratitude for the hobbies and interests you have that make life so much fun—take a moment to write out your thoughts on how old days bring comfort to you.

Journal questions:

- What makes you feel safe?
- What do you fear and why?
- Where are you wanting to grow, but not put in the effort?
- What mental debris is in your way of accomplishing your personal best?
- When did you experience joy today?
- Is there someone you need to forgive?
- What are you most proud of?
- What is something you will never forget?
- Who or what inspires you the most?
- What are your strengths? What are your weaknesses?

(15)

Our Storms

My gran always used to say, "To all souls, the rain must fall." Learning to push our-selves to our limits, to endure the storms that we must all suffer through, is power-ful. People are searching to get out of suffering, and the only way we can get out is by moving forward. It is perseverance of body, heart, mind, and soul to seek the end from the beginning.

There are moments we get that are blissful, then out of the blue something spins us. Calm and peaceful waters turn into chaos, and within a second a storm blows in, drowning us.

How many times do we try to drown out the pain that surrounds us instead of going into the depths of darkness to sob?

That is what the dark night of the soul feels like, and it is almost always brought on by someone or something that shatters our souls open. The storms that we go through, the bolts of lightning that rip through the sky, are the most unexpected moments that we would never ask for.

Throughout my years of coaching, I never once knew what it meant to be so terri-fied of what was happening around me as I did during a USA development camp in Lamoni, Iowa. It was the day of the lightning storm. We had just finished training and began our walk back to the dorms in a light rain. Out of nowhere, lightning bolts began to strike the ground around us. I knew we had to get the kids and ourselves out of harm's way, but I didn't know how. We didn't know when or where each bolt would hit. The rain was pouring, the lightning bolts were striking, and all we could do was run. Our bodies were moving in unison, and I believe God had us in a mirac-ulous flow of the kids and coaches, lighting and thunder, and it was a miracle that no one was struck. Everyone went into a phase of survival and began to be one with Source and a natural knowing of where the next lightning bolt would strike. What I

"And once the storm is over,

you won't remember how you made it through,

how you managed to survive.

You won't even be sure whether the storm is over.

But one thing is certain.

When you come out of the storm,

you won't be the same person who walked in.

That's what this storm's all about."

—Haruki Murakami

learned on this day was that when we are in pure alignment with Source, we will be okay. There was no rhyme or reason why we had success that day other than none of us were destined to die that day. There was too much lightning and too many kids to experience that miracle without it being the will of Source.

Life is everything that this storm had to offer. From sun rays and white clouds to rain, thunder, and lightning. The storms of our journey come, and often they come hard and fast. We grow through the process of planting and replanting our seeds, we climb through the mountains, and embark on the journey through our ocean of mind, but all the while, we deal with these spurts of storms throughout our lives.

Everyone needs to know the rain is coming, because without it we will never know what a bright day looks like. We will never know what it means to be grateful to be alive in this moment, this day. Shit has happened in my life, and God has balanced it with an amazing abundance of blessings and bliss. How awesome it is to know that sunshine and rain will always have their fair share of balance in our lives? Giving gratitude to both is a blessing. Being able to say that I am breathing gives me the blessing that this is the best day of my life.

Don't be that person who thinks about taking away life. Be the one to tell yourself and others that for every day the lightning storm hits, there are a hundred days of sunshine on the way. Not every day needs to be a struggle. If we focus on all the sunshine of today, yesterday, and tomorrow, the storms that come throughout our lives will not be magnified bigger than necessary. We get to choose to focus our minds on creating brighter days. The next bright day is just around the corner, and too many people are giving up in the middle of the storm.

If the dark clouds are here or are coming shortly, *do not quit*. You can and will see the sun again. The cure for quitting is to turn your eyes upon Source, which is pure love. Find one person, then two, then three, and tell them how much you love them and appreciate them. Go out in the neighborhood and do something kind for another person. Pick up trash along each path you walk. Do anything to release the natural doses of love, kindness, and purpose. Make your life a giving tree that is always in bloom. I promise you these acts will shorten the rain storms, and not allow the lightning to strike you on top of the head.

I've had moments where I have told myself, *I quit. I don't want to play*. But I have considered others over myself, and each time it has led me to show up for another until I could show up again for myself. I hope you learn from this book that we are too brave to not keep writing the rest of our stories.

Your story is your masterpiece, live it to the end.

Yes, there have been times when I felt overwhelmed with the losses I went through, but no matter what, I always think I can win, even when it's 24-0. Experts at life are those who can stay in the game and still get their ass kicked. Why am I qualified to write this book? Because I have had my ass kicked, my businesses destroyed, and family taken from me in the most terrible ways. My life is no different from yours because we all suffer through storms; we all have the same stories of trials and tribulations. We all learned to endure. We all have scars on our butts from life's whippings. The scars are our visual reminder of how freaking strong and capable we are of weathering the worst storms.

This is what I have taught my athletes to know and understand: As much as you think you are alone—*you are not*. There are teams of souls everywhere seeking connection and direction throughout our lives, but we must reach out. Even my players who are not playing for me anymore reach out to me in search of guidance because none of us can navigate by ourselves. We need each other. People who can be a guide in someone's life are like the buoys that bob along in the middle of the ocean. You and I are more than capable of offering help to those who are seeking a listening ear. We get to be the buoys for each other, so that when we find ourselves stranded in an ocean of darkness and a storm of defeats, we can reach out and ask for help too. These were the same words I spoke to a former player of mine as she sat at my kitchen table sobbing because of how alone she felt. As I comforted her and asked her to speak about the thoughts swimming in her head, a lot of what was hurting began to surface. She then read me a passage from her journal, which said: "I get so lonely I sometimes feel totally alone and unloved. It makes we want to die." This precious moment of vulnerability from this young player of mine was a gift from God. It unveiled a truth that so many of us need to hear, which is when we feel like we are drowning, but we are willing to be vulnerable, we are giving that opportunity to let that pain be heard. We give ourselves a chance to survive the storms. How many people are we encountering on the street, in the hallways, at the store, who are all feeling that same ache, but not feeling heard?

The answer is everyone. As we sat and cried together, I said, "Look at what a blessing your life is that you can say these words to someone, 'I am worthy of speaking to you because *I am you*.'"

When she began to cast her thoughts into her journal, she asked Source to find someone to hear her needs. My hope is that every one of us can be a buoy in someone's life. That they can pick up the phone and call in their deepest and darkest moments. This moment between me and my player was worth everything I have suffered through because I was able to help her navigate her storm. I know I am a good volleyball coach, but the game has allowed me to become a great life coach. Without the experiences of coaching hundreds of teams to success, I would not have learned how to coach those souls to success. I get to lead others from a place of pure love, knowing that everyone is a champion waiting to be given permission to rise. I get to be there for all my kids, to love them so much that I can discipline them, disagree with them, and hold them to a standard that is above and beyond anything they dreamed possible. This also requires that I allow them to hold me to the highest standards of leadership. Sports have allowed me to show kids we can all do hard things and win the game called life.

As I look back over my reputation as a hard ass coach, I am a firm believer that that was part of what made me successful. My athletes believed we were all doing something really important with life's precious hours. I always knew that we could

Reflection:

Have you helped someone today?

triumph over any weakness and return back to our infinite power. If we do not teach resilience through sport and through life, then young kids and adults will quit when the going gets tough. Demanding excellence creates high levels of self-confidence and efficacy. Never fear the old-school philosophies around demanding our excellences. We all deserve that love and it is not mean-spirited to expect it.

It is difficult to search for meaning when you spiral to the darkest places of defeat. Down in these deep, dark currents and storms are when you must realize you've hit a danger zone. This place on the raging sea is when we must seek professional help immediately. There are so many lighthouses of hope to help you out of the raging sea, but it starts with telling someone how you feel.

Whatever experience you're suffering through, love yourself enough to feel the damn thing. Feel it. Be it. So that it does not become the death of your soul. Enough of those shattered pieces called memories, pain, heartache—everything that gets suppressed in the silence of our souls.

Please don't become silent; it is deadly. Speak about what is hurting you. Flow through what you go through. Do not let these storms destroy you from the inside out. It's why, as spirit beings, we came and chose to have this human experience. We chose to go through the rain instead of watching it rain. Source is here with us, guiding us with every step we take. So many times I have found myself alone, speaking with God and saying, "I know you got me. I know that at the end of this journey, there is light. But I am tired." Here is what I have learned in this repetitive prayer of mine: Nobody gets to go to God unannounced. Through the despair and dark storms, will come a light of hope.

> ## Whatever experience you are suffering through, love yourself enough to feel the damn thing. Feel it. Be it.

My hope for all of us is that when we get to those places of darkness and despair, we will become extremely brave and reach out to someone and talk it through. Take that step of courage—you are absolutely worth it. What can we say in the darkest times to ourselves and to each other? This too will pass, but I am here for you until it does. Focus on the things you can control—your thoughts. Choose thoughts that create forward movement out of the situation. Focus on one good, amazing thing in your life, even if the only thing you can find is that your heart is beating and that you are able to breathe.

This is the look of the lighthouse. Through the deep ocean of our mind, when we are at sea being thrown and thrashed, there is but a small ray of light in the distance, waiting to guide us back in after we've felt so lost, so tired, and so alone. It is calling us through the darkness saying, "Hold on. I am with you always, and I will never test you more than you can handle. I am going to keep you afloat until you can gather yourself and weather the storm." That is Source's promise.

> **Heaven is a consistent choice. In every moment there can be bliss, in every moment there can also be hell. Through some of our deepest sorrows will come our greatest joys.**

Lesson Sixteen
Life Time-Out

Purpose: To give your body, mind, and spirit time to rest, rejuvenate, restore, reflect, and recover. Life time-outs occur for connections. Find ways to completely disconnect from the hustle and bustle of daily life. Intentionally disconnect for a few days. Learn to relax and enjoy life's time-outs. Find a few ideas that will inspire you into relaxation during vacations or staycations.

Tools:
- Your imagination
- Books

Activity: Try different ways to disconnect with the business of life and reconnect with yourself. The following are some examples:

Read a good book. A few great recommendations:

The Power of Intention by Dr. Wayne Dyer
A New Earth by Eckhart Tolle
The Mastery of Love by Don Miguel Ruiz
The Power of TED by David Emerald
Daring Greatly by Dr. Brené Brown

- Take a walk around the vacation area and experience art. It could be a fountain in a park or a painting in an art studio.
- Walk barefoot in the sand or grass. Feel the grounding that occurs when we connect with nature.
- Take a mindful breathing walk. On the inhale, say, "I am love." On the exhale, breathe out all the stress.
- Schedule a massage and/or spa day.
- Take a swim in the pool or ocean.
- Go on a scenic drive.

"How beautiful it is to do nothing, and then rest afterwards."

—Spanish proverb

Part Four

For Our Souls

Our Lighthouse

If our minds are an ocean of thoughts, then what is the way out when we get lost at sea? I've always believed that the journey to empowerment is the journey to finding your pure Source of light. The ray of guidance from a lighthouse gives any human being hope when experiencing darkness in a raging sea. In moments that shatter us and when we think of memories that make us feel like we are drowning, sometimes our compass and map are not enough to get us through. Everyone needs a Source. Everyone needs a ray of guidance from the lighthouse. It is our purest form of direction when we are lost.

We talk about the journey from here to there, as the path weaves in and out of various terrains. We are born, planting the first seeds in

Our Life's Garden. From our garden, we venture out to live and grow through the ups and downs that life has to offer—*Our Mountains and Valleys.* We collect moments, memories, and lessons that root and blossom with every step we take. We come to shores that lead to oceans, and in every path we choose, there are storms we must endure. The times when we are not only fighting to survive through the terrain of our realities, but we're also dealing with the trials that come to test us—the trials that seek to destroy the paths we have journeyed through.

As we enter "Part Four: For Our Souls—Our Lighthouse," we reflect back on *who we are* and *who we want to become.* I need you to trust yourself and trust your Source. Whether it is God, Universe, Cosmos, Energy, Mother Nature, or any other form, ask your Source to be here with you in this moment and in every moment to come. It will be your guide. It will be your lighthouse.

Chapters

---

(16)

Our Paths

At this point in *Our Soul's Journey*, we can imagine ourselves swimming and floating to the shore where the lighthouse rests. Our body, heart, and mind are all exhausted by repeated swims during the big storms, and at the same time, we have experienced the bliss of life's many blessings. We now gather our wisdom and soul muscle that has been strengthened by life's trialed swims. We know we can do hard things; we know our Source is with us always and the journey gets exciting.

In the moments our lives encounter the raging seas, be assured that the struggle will bring us all to our destination. This destination will not be an accident or a mistake; it will always bring us to a place meant for us. We learn to trust with great faith that our purpose will always align with the path we are on right here, right now! It takes courage to rebuild our mindset each day with words, actions, and deeds that align with the current most likely to bring us to our journey's desired end.

When we get into those spaces where it is dark and cloudy, and we don't know what direction to go, that's when things become scary. Everyone is on this crashing course headed out to sea, back to Source, back to soul. Deliverance only happens through living it and crossing it; we must swim through it to get to the other side. None of us go exempt, unless you are the innocent child born so perfectly that God returns you home. The rest of us get to embark on this long and sometimes lonely journey from the garden through mountains and valleys, across the sea back to the lighthouse. Every step or misstep is a part of our life's path.

In reality, passion and purpose are found along the winding journey. We often don't know what these are until we dream our first dream and see the destination, and most times just prior to our arrival, life's detours send our path to purpose in a completely different direction. God will give us a matched blessing that will hold us up and help us be who we were meant to be. The truth is, we become the best versions of ourselves after something refines us. Grace, empathy, and forgiveness are

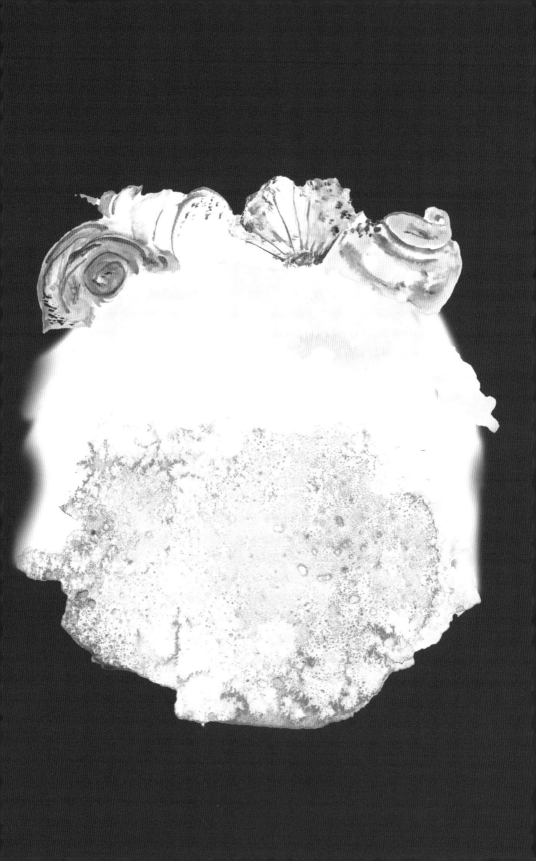

the antidotes for healing the blisters we experience on the longer hikes or swims we were not prepared for. The promise is that we will all arrive at our destination according to the divine plan of servitude, passion, and purpose.

I know for me, had I not suffered through these trials, I would not have known when the blessing of my God's love arrived. There are significant times in a person's life when something absolutely soul wrenching occurs, and you just don't know how much further you can go. This usually involves encountering or dealing with the death of a loved one, the death of a dream, or the death of yourself in some form. It is a time where a person might decide that they cannot go any longer.

At twenty-one years old, I experienced my first significant loss of a life buoy. My gran died suddenly and without warning. She was my anchor; the one who stabilized the blinking buoy during the raging seas. She had a massive heart attack during her afternoon coffee. She was young, only sixty-three, and she was my world! My gran exuded love, kindness, and compassion. She witnessed unconditional love daily. I did not understand grief, but I remember feeling so lost, angry, and abandoned at sea. My tether had snapped, and I wanted God to bring her back to me. The last memory I have of my gran was her telling me she was so proud that I was getting my college degree that June and reminded me that "opportunities and doors that were open for girls were not open for her generation." I took her words and decided that I would build a legacy for her love, strength, and compassion. I often check my life by asking Gran if my life has made her proud.

> **I know for me, had I not suffered through these trials I would not have known when the blessing of my God's love arrived.**

Fast forward some years to 2011—another point in my life where I was questioning life's raging sea. I was lonely and wondering if I would ever find a soulmate. Multiple category four hurricanes blasted through my life, but thankfully between the coming of the other three storms, God brought me an angel to swim with me when I thought I was drowning. Miracles sometimes come as tender mercies that keep us afloat during the excruciating pain of grief from loss.

Shortly after her arrival in my life, my father died, stripping away another major anchor in my life. By 2013, I had lost $250,000 in failed investments. I was forced to resign as CEO of an organization I had built over twenty-five years out of blood, sweat, and tears; and within months of this devastating loss, I was fired from my college coaching position.

Everything that was endured during that time of my life was a part of the awakening of coming through the dark night of my soul and seeing what I had become. At the time, my being was anchored in what I was having and doing; I was equating who I was with what I did. I didn't recognize myself by the time I noticed where I was on the journey.

Who was I when I lost everything?

It was one of my greatest storms, because when I was let go as the head coach of the college, I could no longer be "what I did." I didn't have the career title—I was no longer wearing the logo shirts, pants, and hoodies that bore the purple crest. I had to sell my dream house and car just to survive. I didn't know who I was anymore, and that brought me to where I am today.

The entire time I was strolling along thinking I had it all; I had no idea what was coming. Today, I know that what came was meant to redirect my path to help me get to a clearer space that gives me the opportunity to be more humble and grateful for every day I am blessed to be here. It was all a part of my path back to purpose. This goes back to the question: In the middle of nowhere with nothing and no one, who are you? If you lose your dream career, house, car, or spouse...who are you?

> **When we become everything outside of our passion and purpose, that is when we lose our lives. We shift into negative ego patterns that move Source's plan for life to unreachable locations.**

That October, just days after I was released as head coach, I found myself in the volleyball gym. Only this time instead of college girls, I was met with a group of young Polynesian athletes. I remember walking into the gym feeling defeated, tired, and sad. A player's mother approached me, and I said these words to her: "I've been fired. You probably don't want me." She looked at me with reassurance saying, "We want you. Nobody else wants us."

I was known to be a crazy coach, and my style was not always the most delightful, but I am competitive. Hell, I grew up with two younger brothers—the only way I could survive my childhood was to be a hard ass and relentless when the going gets tough. As I began to mentor this group of Polynesian girls, I realized that my method of coaching lined up with morals. They were raised in a culture that respected their elders and knew of discipline and hard work. They became my extended family along with loyal players who left the program at the college where I

was released. These groups of women became the tribe who did not abandon me during my darkest times.

I began coaching up these girls, relaunching High Country Volleyball, and building a team of players who would represent the state of Utah at the American Samoa Bowl Games. Over the next few months leading into December, we began mapping out our training schedule, practices, and fundraising events that would take us across the Pacific Ocean to Samoa. When I arrived on the island, I felt a connection to the people and ambience of the culture. It felt like *magic*.

Even though I was alone and without my family for the first Christmas ever, I was surrounded by my new family and friends. I met people who offered me a sense of guidance and peace. I became extremely ill on this beautiful island with a fever well over a 103°F. The family brought over an old Samoan medicine woman who healed my body. As she began to rub ointments over my body, I remember her telling me that my illness was not physical, but rather a spiritual sickness. She told me that I was sick with grief and my soul was broken. This woman glowed and her spirit exuded a lighthouse of love. As she began touching my skin, she spoke and said, "You are here to do God's work." I felt healed almost immediately. The heaviness of defeat, hurt, loss, and sadness began to leave my body, heart, mind, and soul. I was sobbing, but I think the tears that were leaving were the pain my body bottled up. I was letting go with every breath I took and trusting that I was exactly where I needed to be—in the middle of the South Pacific Ocean with an angel who led me back from the raging sea.

I believe that God sent me to Samoa during that time of my life for a reason. It was all a part of this divine design to guide me back to my path of purpose. He sent me back to my roots. Though I cannot trace any lineage to Samoa, there was something there that told me I was home. The people of the island showed me a love that was unconditional, and that was my first step toward home on the journey from life's storms.

Every answer to our questions has always been right there, hidden in each step that you and I have taken throughout this journey. When we're not living on purpose, and we get distracted, we end up not doing our best work because our attention is everywhere else besides the right here, right now.

Even my set of angel cards have said to me: "Get right with yourself, and everything else will flow." It is the entire process of healing every part of who I am in body, heart, mind, and soul. A lot of our issues come from the parts that we wish to hide, bury, or drown. The honest truth is that we will not become the most amazing version of ourselves when hiding from the most painful pieces of our past or present.

Take the broken pieces of ourselves, reevaluate them, reassess them, and ask why they came and bless them with love and forgiveness. We get permission to break down and build back up. It is the beauty of waking up each day with twenty-four hours to heal, grow, flow, learn, and laugh. Nobody gave me a manual when I came out of the womb saying to just toughen up and suppress. Hell yeah, we're tough, but we're also human beings with beating hearts and minds that wander.

> **Get out of ego, and get into spirit because the hardest part of our life is overcoming the fear of giving ourselves our all— being the healthiest we can be physically, emotionally, mentally, and spiritually.**

People say to just move on, put it all aside, and handle your shit, but at some point that becomes toxic. Toxic to you and to those you love. We don't need to be hiking up our paths with extra rocks and weight in our pockets or purposely cross into dangerous currents. Rather, we have the chance and the choice to flow into the moment we are in, take life time-outs, and give ourselves a second to breathe and rejuvenate. Life is hard, and the path can be strenuous.

There will be an abundance of trials we will endure, and I promise it'll all be for our greater good. As we learn the lessons meant for us, we'll be able to navigate all of the storms perfectly and humbly. Stay strong, walk on—it's time to get back on our path. Get on purpose. When you think it and it becomes, that is when Source is vibrating at manifesting speeds with the Universe. Build a life that serves Source's needs and the needs of our planet.

Through trials like these, we cannot pretend nothing is happening. Everything just is. It all flows in and out, comes and goes. The emotions catch up with us bringing a deep sorrow of loss and despair. We need to let it flow like water. For me, these were devastations where I was not sure if I could get out of bed, far less swim another day. I had physical responses where I thought I was dying . . . and a part of me was. Loss and change was happening; I was experiencing the death of the old me. What was occurring was the death of the egoic part of me that did not work. There are many successful parts of the ego that assist us in many ways, but the ones that edge God out are not what I wanted in my life anymore. I wanted true happiness. I was my creation, and I was also the only one hiking this path. I got to find my soul on this journey that now is full of humble gratitude for all those who played a role in creating the story of the end, which is the beginning.

It is time that you, my friends, look within yourself to see where you are on the journey. Do not circulate yourself in spaces that rotate negative vibrations. If there are weeds that need to be removed, canyons meant to climb out of, or oceans of thoughts that need to be swam through, please do it. Do it for yourself, for your family and friends. Make that journey of self-discovery. You will be amazed at what you will find.

Everything around us is here for a short moment. Our lives are meant to be pursued with those that can support us as we all walk the path. No one is exempt from loss. If there is anything that I wish for us to learn, it is the lesson of grief. When life is altered, every one of us has to go through the grace and gift of grieving the loss of a loved one, career, pet, friend, sport, partner, or career. The list goes on and on about the people or things we all miss or lose. People are in such a rush to move on with their lives, but the healing process is messy. We all know that. We all feel that. Our world teaches us that there's no time to waste, or tears to be shed—how far from the truth that is. Most people stay stuck in the denial and anger phases of their lives, because they do not know how to deal with the loss of themselves, people, things, or moments. You and I can choose differently.

Grief is very personal; it follows no rules or schedules and creates a hole in the soul that only time can and will heal. The path that it follows goes something like this: shock and denial, pain and guilt, anger and bargaining, depression, and then a re-construction of your life filled with hope and acceptance.

Don't be fooled into thinking there's something wrong with you after you have loved, toiled, and committed your life to something that really matters. We all have endured terrible tribulations. Parents who have to grieve their empty nests. People who have lost their jobs. Athletes who can no longer play the sport they dedicated their lives to. Children who lose beloved grandparents. Turbulence is the cause of our paths being directed to new places, places you and I have never been before, but until we can understand grief and what it looks and feels like, we will never know how to move forward on our journeys.

Take the life time-outs you need to heal yourself, body, heart, mind, and soul. Usually when you lose a loved one or a life partner, most people understand the time that is needed to heal. But losing your job, business, or pet may be different; people may not give grace or the time needed for healing. Take it anyway because life is too short to live with a broken soul. We all deserve light, love, and true happiness.

Everyone deserves to grieve any death they experience, because death is not only the physical burying of a person, but it could also be the metaphorical burying of one's self. Whether that's weeds you continue to ignore, feelings that you seek to hide, or memories you wish to escape from. It only matters that here and now you face it all. Grieve the hurt that was brought to you through these life storms. Work through that depression, and get to a place of hope and acceptance.

There will be an abundance of trials we will endure, and I promise it'll all be for our greater good. As we learn the lessons meant for us, we'll be able to navigate all of the storms humbly. Stay strong, and walk on—it's time to get back on our path. Get on with your purpose. Build a life that serves Source's needs and the needs of our planet.

Life sometimes will feel like a plateau—the flat line on a heart reading or a recurring current that's got you stuck. There will be moments where we are out in the middle of nowhere and we wonder if we are going anywhere; those places are terrifying. In these spaces where we're not sure where to go, the only confidence we have is to trust ourselves and trust our Source. Even in the most traumatizing moments when we just don't know how much further we can go, we must believe that our Source will carry us precisely where we are meant to be.

> **Have the courage to pursue your dream board, and the patience to understand that none of it is on our time. Through every trial, Heaven is coming. Just one more step. One more climb. One more stroke back to light and love.**

"My precious child,

I love you and I would never leave you. During your times of trial and suffering, when you saw only one set of footprints in the sand, it was then that I carried you."

—Margaret Fishback

Lesson Seventeen
Calm Before the Storms

Purpose: Trying to sleep amidst life tragedies is so hard, but it is so necessary and restorative. However, don't let depression keep you in bed; build a routine that clearly outlines the appropriate times for rest and stillness. Implementing sleep routines is important. Creating a space and time frame that allows your body, heart, mind, and soul to feel calmness and peace is essential to overall well-being. This lesson is used to implement new bedtime habits to assist you with deep sleep to restore your energy for your active times.

Activity: Improve your sleep routines and restoration by trying out some of the following options.

Anchor Sleep Habits: Most people set an alarm to wake up, but now we're going to try setting an alarm to go to sleep. We should create a consistent sleep pattern by going to bed and waking at the same times each and every day. Yes, even on holidays and weekends.

Room Temperature: Sleeping in a cold room is very beneficial; the temperature tells the body to rest. We should have the room around 65°F.

Darkness: Our bodies produce melatonin as the lights go down. Work to reduce bright lighting in the house as you prepare for sleep; turn off screens and phones. It is also very helpful to have blackout curtains or tinted windows.

Walk It Out: If you wake in the middle of the night and cannot go back to sleep, after about twenty-five minutes get up, write, meditate, and reset yourself. Return to bed when you feel sleepy. We can train our bodies so that bed is a consistent place for sleep.

Eliminate Caffeine: Eliminate your use of caffeine late in the day as well as any type of stimulant that does not allow the body to begin its nightly wind down. Also, a little alcohol is okay, but getting really tipsy before bed can cause sleep pattern interruptions.

Develop a Wind-Down Routine: A wind-down routine is like landing a plane; it slowly and gradually gets yourself ready for sleep. It involves creating habits that relax and slow the thinking process. During breakup and trauma situations, the brain loves to continually repeat the same scenarios over and over again. Work hard to redirect the mind to your love and gratitude list. Repeat the items on your list over and over again, reminding yourself what we are thankful for and people who bring us great love and joy.

"Trust in the Lord with all your heart and lean not on your own understanding."

-Proverbs 3:5

Our Lighthouse

I was exactly where I needed to be as J. E. Fields jumped off the I-80 freeway overpass bridge on my way to the airport. This woman landed on the roadway below, breaking multiple bones just prior to my arrival on the scene. It was February 2014, and I had just returned home from the South Pacific. Once again, an angel sent me, or rather, dropped right out of the sky in front of my car. This woman was trying to end her life, and I was the first responder to assist her on her journey home. I think about this tragedy, and how if it had happened sooner in my life, I would not have been equipped with the necessary strength, faith, or power to look at her broken body and soul to say, "Do you know you are loved by God? The angels have come to carry you home."

As I dialed 911, I learned so many amazing things about this woman. She had society's status symbol for wealth with a platinum American Express credit card. She was a highly educated professor at a nearby university. Her photo ID told me her age, birthdate, and address. This was a successful woman.

I asked her why she jumped. She told me she was lonely, and that her children had moved away, and she had no one who loved her. She was retired, alone, and afraid. You would think this woman had it all. But what she did not have was the hope or love to want to live another day. She jumped off that bridge longing to belong. This is what Dr. Brené Brown has researched and teaches in her books that we will die without belonging and connection. But this is what you and I need to know today:

> **That you are loved, you belong and you matter. We become lost without direction when we do not seek help from Source or others to help us along the way.**

Peace of Mind

People can endure anything that life tosses their way if they know that they are loved, supported, and belong. I am so thankful I have had such amazing souls walking with me during the hard times. We have become a society that has forgotten these basics, these essentials to our survival. We pick up our phones every second of every day seeking out connection and love from people who are not there. We need people to look deeply into our eyes and make that connection. We need souls next to us, the ones who walk beside us, to say, "I love you, and I am here for you." If we could offer any sort of light to those who are lost in the darkness, whether we are the buoys in the middle of nowhere with the flashing red glow that signals, "You are almost there," or we help them to see or hear the ray of guidance, the light from their Source to find the path home.

I've always had a fascination with the lighthouse. A tall, beautiful structure that is built to warn sea travelers of the rocks below, saying the shore is close and you are almost home. It is always there, always shining, leading you back to safety. When I launched the *Empowerment Journey* and my life-coaching business, I knew that the lighthouse would be our foundation. It is a magnificent design set to guide anyone who is lost.

The lighthouse is our most divine Source; it is the essence of joy, love, and peace. Many will ask, "What is the essence of that being—God, Source, Universe?" For me, I believe we know when we feel *it*. It is a universal, all-encompassing feeling. There is a moment when it is pure bliss, and everything around us feels perfect, whole, and complete. It could be after a delicious meal shared with family and friends, or while you're driving down the freeway listening to your favorite song with a splash of orange and pink as your sunset backdrop. There could be endless, small experiences that confirm the existence of a being who is so loving and so powerful that lives within and around us. Source is everywhere. It is everything and it is us.

When we meet these moments along our journey, the level of happiness can be so strong, our bodies cannot contain it. It is that space where we leave the body, we leave the mind, and we truly become a pure soul. It does not matter how anyone defines it, but that essence of being is where we find peace.

Even in those spaces where I feel like I'm not grounded anywhere, I am learning to come to peace with everything that whirls in or around me. To wake up each day never knowing what those twenty-four hours will bring is nerve-racking, but it matters how you trust your Source today. No matter where you are, even if you feel completely alone, Source will send exactly what you need. Every time we get lost along the way, we need to learn to ask Source: "What's next? Where do I go from here?" because I believe Source is all-knowing and desires only what is best for us. The way our lives come together is not how we always imagine it will be, but the way it happens, when it happens, is the beauty of it all. It has no rhyme and no reason, but it is perfect.

Daily, I choose courage, bravery, and confidence with God's divine competence. My healing is a testament to Source's pure love, promise, and devotion. My readers get to see God pour out from my words on paper. Words that declare everything is happening to you, for you. Take your life into your amazing power, believe you can, and you will create your life mission.

I am living and breathing true emotion knowing the pain the world is going through. God always blesses my life with just enough. Just enough hope, pain, love, and disappointment. I am never tested more than I can handle, but I am always blessed. You can find that blessing every day. It is my choice, your choice, and our choice to voice infinite possibility. The past shows us how we made the journey from climbing the highest peaks, to swimming the most difficult of seas. Here is the good news: we can do it.

In moments when I feel completely broken, I pray out loud: "God, you do not need to allow anymore ass kicking. I am looking up to you. I surrender." Source, God, or Universe is that beam of light that shines through the fog, rain, storm, and raging ocean. It is all around us, leading us out of the dark spaces that we all encounter. Humbling ourselves to ask for the help we need does not make us weak. It makes us human.

None of us can venture on this path alone; we need each other, and we need our Source. In fact, our biggest journey is our greatest discovery of love today. Love for ourselves and love for others. The more we can do in life outside of judgement and outside of hate to be more in love, the better we will be. We must ask ourselves if our response to others is loving and kind. And we need to ask ourselves if the response to us is loving and kind. If poison is killing off our garden path or spreading into our hearts and minds, it clouds our direction. Creating a bond with your Source—to know and trust that you are one, your body, heart, mind, and soul—will naturally follow the beam of light that presses through darkness.

Everyone's got advice for us, but at the end of the day, you've got to trust what you know and what Source is telling you. Do not betray your spiritual wisdom. All this time, I have been really pushing to find an answer to everything and God has now said: "I've got this. Let go, and let me do my work, because you are getting off path spending all your mental time with the same 60,000 thoughts of your ex-love, career hardships, stress, and worry, and I'm asking you for 75,000 thoughts on pure love

"In order for the light

to shine so brightly,

the darkness must

be present."

–Francis Bacon

and faith. Focus on the power I have to heal and guide you through this. I am your lighthouse."

> **Everyone's got advice for us, but at the end of the day, you've got to trust what you know and what Source is telling you. Do not betray your spiritual wisdom.**

We get to get out of the way of God's magnificence and let Heaven be created through us here on Earth.

Let God's love for you be created through you to the world. You will never be tested more than you can handle. Have a mindset focused on tiny steps toward changing your world. As we begin to change our world, the world changes. Believe in the perfect adventure of life, let God be God. If pure Source is in you, then you are pure Source. What amazing power you have with this knowing. You've got unlimited abundance right here, right now. Please choose to live, love, and forgive. It is always about forgiving yourself first; you did the best you could with what you knew. Grace for the past, and conscious purpose for the future.

In time, all things will be revealed. The hardest thing I have had to do lately amidst the pandemic is take a moment to breathe and say, "God, your will, your way." It's in the surrender that I have learned the most. Every day needs to be a constant question of what brings us a high vibration and gives us the energy and peace we have on our good days. How can you and I recreate those moments over and over again to then build the best version of our lives?

Reflect. Pray. Meditate. Journal. Dream board. Visualize.

We all have access to that realm. It is why we pray to put us in a spiritual realm. Mediation and ancient teachings of how humans spoke to the other side for guidance has been people's way of life since the beginning of time. We can see it in yoga, meditation, walkabouts, and chants. There are all kinds of ways that people have gotten spiritually connected, but finding what works for *you* is so important. Everything we wish to become starts within us and our belief to know that Source is our lighthouse. It will guide us throughout our entire journey, from beginning to end.

I know there is a thin, distinct veil between Heaven and Earth. Nothing happens without an equal and opposite reaction and response that is in perfect synchronicity within the planet. I have spoken out loud and manifested magical moments time and time again. I manifested the blessing of angels, and they have been with me on my journey to empowerment. Growing up, my mom was raised Catholic, but she went through a phase as an agnostic. She knew the power of both the dark and light sides. We come from a legacy of gypsies and clairvoyance. As a young child, I made my mother afraid because I would cry and yell that I wanted to go back to God. I knew spirits well, and I could see them. It frightened many that I knew things before they happened, and I could see the other side; I would experience spiritual awakenings, even at a young age.

The big picture is—we come through our parents. Not of them. At a spiritual level, the 1 in 400 trillion chance of our birth starts the journey we are going to take; the path we take will lead us back to that lighthouse and place where we will grow to become who we were always meant to be. From the garden to the lighthouse—and everything in between—we will learn to be one with ourselves and one with our Sources.

As a Capricorn, I am a sea goat and a mountain goat. Both goats are not isolated in either the mountains or the sea. It is a voyage to the mountains and back to the sea that makes us who we are. The year 2020 was one of great triumph and transformation for everyone, and so much of what we have been through has been about *Our Soul's Journey*, pulling us back to Source, to the lighthouse.

I believe that everything happens for a reason. Those things, people, and moments that go from A to B to C to Z are in a divine plan, created for each soul walking on their journey. Years ago my dad said, "When you find peace, peace will come. It will come and everything will flow," he pointed up to the moon and said, "You see that full moon? That light of the moon and the light of the sun will never cease to exist to be the light."

The lighthouse is the same. Whether it is the sun, moon, God, Universe, or Cosmos, the lighthouse is with us always. It will never cease to exist and will forever lead us back to shore after you and I have been lost.

"Like a guardian angel, the lighthouse stands, sending out hope in the night.

Like a faithful friend reaching out a hand, bringing comfort, truth, and light."

–Unknown

Lesson Eighteen
Lighthouse Lesson

Purpose: Take a moment to bask in the sunlight or the glow of the moon. Concentrate on the gravity that pulls you to the Earth, and trust that your lighthouse will guide you from beginning to end. As a teacher of the lighthouse, it is important to guide students through the learning process, just as the lighthouse helps the sailors at sea, this memoir will only assist you if you do the work.

Knowing that you are the light of your house. What you think first is what happens next. Learning to mediate on your creations is the most powerful visualization you can do. Putting the passion and purpose to your mediations coupled with the *energy* of excitement, thrill, and exaltation makes it happen. You cannot worry if you focus your mind on your creations of success. Mediation eliminates worries, anxieties, and other negative feelings because you cannot be miserable and happy at the same time.

Tools:
- Dream board

Activity: Take time to reconnect with items on your dream board and focus on allowing those realities into your life.

step one:
Look at a picture on your dream board and focus the intentions of
that piece on your board. Take a moment to breathe for one minute in a room of silence. Time yourself.

step two:
After the minute is complete, add five more minutes to the clock. Allow your mind, heart, body, and soul to detox from anything that feels heavy.

step three:
Each day, continue this cycle, and add five minutes until you are able to meditate for thirty whole minutes in one sitting.

For each five-minute block, focus on different item. Example: Take five minutes to release something stressful, five minutes to show gratitude for a person, five minutes to practice "I love" statements, and maybe five minutes to practice "I am" statements. Break it up, and release and attract everything you want.

Our Life's Forest

With every place we have been, we encounter dark moments. It is in the deepest moments of despair that our lighthouse is the brightest. In the storms and winds, it remains there, calling us back to land, calling us back in after we've been lost.

One of my most favorite authors, Dr. Wayne Dyer, said, "An infinity of forest lies dormant within the dreams of one acorn." Dormant forces lie deeply hidden within each of us, just like that acorn. But do you know what it takes to open that acorn? An intense fire, because an acorn shell won't crack until it is blazing hot. The rains from a storm grow us, while the intense fires of everything we have suffered through break open the magical seed within us. The heat is so strenuous that the acorn bursts to create a forest.

Everything you and I suffer through leads to the crescendo to discovering the seed of an acorn, the very first seed of *who we are* when we come to this Earth. It was within us all along as we journeyed from there to here. And all the while, we became not just a garden, but a *forest* of our transformations, self-discoveries, thoughts, and memories. We can take a look back at the path we journeyed through to see a trail of memories and lessons marking who we were and who we became. We can see all the way back to our first flower and weed. The plants sprinkled along the path; the weeds that we replanted; the trees that became a part of our forest. It is all there, rooted along the journey leading to the lighthouse.

Transformation and *experience* could be the same word. Without the experience of success, we don't know where we come from, and without the experience of failure, we don't know what we can do. In the journey to true transformation, the experience will only build you for that moment to prepare you for the storms that will come again. The difference is, as we get older, we gain wisdom and scars, and those scars remind us that as much as we've been bruised and defeated, we will find success on the other side again.

We must all learn how to create the winner within us who grows brighter through each success. Allow yourself space to hear the inner voice, eliminate the noise for a while, and connect and affect change. Put your hands on the Earth. Plant seeds of love, joy, and hope. Follow your path through your mountain and valley and have the faith to embark on your journey across the ocean of your mind.

Each of us gets to blaze the path with our complete and focused passion to get back on purpose. The secret is simple: Fall in love with yourself and be able to love everything and forgive. Until we forgive, we can't love. We can't forget what happened or what was said because it's etched there forever, but forgiveness is always the replacement of hatred and hurt. Even as Christ was dying on the cross, He had these final words: "Lord, forgive them for they know not what they do." God's example to me has been my greatest Source of light and love. God has walked this journey with me, even though there were times it felt like I was walking alone. Source is the lighthouse leading us all back home.

At the end of the day, sure, we can grow a garden with some rain and some seeds, but we can't blossom into a thicket of trees, full of life and potential without the hottest of fires. The biggest question that we must get into a routine of asking ourselves every damn day has got to be: *What do I want in this life?*

Do we want a big forest that is deep rooted? Or do we just want a perennial garden? All this time, all these years, I was so afraid of being alone, but when I let go of everything—the pain, anguish, expectation, and fear—the beauty of my life came to fruition. I really do believe that our perfect life is waiting for each of us to surrender to our Sources and let the lighthouse guide us back in from our sea of sorrow, pain, loss, and everything holding us back from living and loving our best selves and our best lives.

You and I are trying to force everything on our dream boards into reality instead of asking Source and soul for the guidance and the purpose for it all. We betray our bodily wisdom by ignoring the model of a perfect spiritual life inside ourselves. Source promises that every need will be met—emotionally, physically, mentally, socially, all of it, if we can only have faith, trust, and endure.

God is the space between all matter, and I am committed to looking at all angles of my life. I will live each day as my last day. No regrets, no time to waste, no person to hold me back. I will relax and let all life flow, rest, feel, and believe that it is all perfect. It is all good. We get to let go and we get to live in spirit with Source because it is always right here—right now in this moment of time.

That's the beauty of every day we wake up. From the minute we came here, we came as a spirit that took on a human form. This journey is returning us back to a spirit form. Ashes to ashes, dust to dust, that is the knowing in the Christian faith—that there is life after death. It gives us that peace that our soul is a piece of the light from the original Source. It is that first seed planted deep within our body, heart, mind, and soul. That essence that glows beneath our skin to show the world who we truly are. It is the magical seed of an acorn that we carry within us, the one that permeates after enduring trials to then flourish into our forest.

We are spirit beings having a human experience. We all have come here with different talents; no two of us are the same. You and I have lived and breathed our triumphs, and because of this, we possess a unique set of experiences and perspectives that differentiate us from other souls. Had we not suffered or endured, we would have never learned. These lessons of life are needed at every aspect of one's journey. They bring balance and provide the toughness that comes from a calm self-assurance, a steady faith in one's abilities, and a firm reliance on one's inner strengths. It is way easier to not live in our divine power, because divine power requires you to trust yourself, and we are all struggling with that truth. The world will tear you down and convince you that you are not enough. Learning how to tap into your power and knowing you are infinitely enough is the purest form of love within ourselves that we can be, do, and have everything we want—so long as we know that everything happens for a reason.

> **The world will tear you down and convince you that you are not enough. Learning how to tap into your power and knowing you are infinitely enough is the purest form of love within ourselves.**

Like magic, that first seed comes to Earth perfect, whole, and complete. It was always there; it has always been; it will always be. As we've agreed to this journey through the garden, through the mountains, through the raging sea, through the hope and turmoil, through peace, labels, and limits...we will all journey back. As much as today feels scary and out of control, we are on our way back to Source. Back to perfect, whole, and complete. I promise you, as you live, love, and endure, your forest is going to blossom beautifully.

Every path we take will lead and guide us back to the Source of the lighthouse. Sure, we start off as a garden with flowers, plants, and weeds. But as we live, learn, and grow, along the way we will gather seeds of hope, peace, love, and joy. It is through *Our Soul's Journey* that we will all blossom to become the magnificent trees of our life where we become who we were meant to be.

Where we become our life's forest.

Lesson Nineteen
Magic Wand

Purpose: Making your magic happen. Not everyone has the luxury of living near a lighthouse, but we do all have access to the outdoors. Go outside and connect with nature! Take a walk through a nearby forest, find a creek, and feel the energy that emulates from every creature or plant and appreciate the life that lives within and around you. Breathe in and out and reflect on your experience.

Put the magic in your hand. Just as Luke Skywalker was given the lightsaber, your wand is what you take into the cave with you. When Luke asked Yoda what was in the cave, Yoda's response was, "What you take in." This is teaching you that the light within is what your wand will magically create.

Tools:
- Stick
- Glue
- Paints
- Markers
- Crystals
- Feathers
- Leaves

Activity: Create a wand to act as a symbol for your light.

step one:
Go outside and find a large stick, then sand it down.

step two:
Color the stick with markers or paint, or you can wrap the stick with reversed packing tape, sticky side out.

step three:
Collect items to paint, glue, or stick to your magic wand. First, pick out a large stick, then sand down your handle. You can paint the stick, glue your favorite crystals on it, add feathers, add leaves, etc. Make it as magical as your imagination will allow.

Our Soul's Journey

Imagine the path. The journey begins as small and simple seeds, both flowers and weeds. As we walk along the path, the seeds grow with every step we walk, and they take root as we move forward in life. The path goes through a mountain of ups and a valley of downs, and it all leads us back out to the shore of sand that stretches out to the depths of our oceans. A place that can get so dark and dangerous, we almost never risk going out there, but the ones who are willing to take a risk and find their way back always come back stronger. Once we've ventured far enough into the ocean of our minds, just to find the pearls of wisdom we were meant to discover, we can add it to our collection of things we have learned throughout life. Though pearls are not seeds, they do offer beautiful markings of what we have found during our adventures. It's like the crystals we discover in the valleys and canyons, or the polished stones from the rivers, the things we collect as we go through our journey. These are what we carry to remember where we have been, and they remind us that there is beauty in where we are going.

With every step we take on our journey, we will see events in our life unfold perfectly and in their own season of harvest. Every weed, canyon, or storm we encounter will all be a part of *Our Soul's Journey*. Becoming who we were meant to be is a long process that requires consistent effort.

> **I have not met one successful person in my life who has not been in the arena and had their ass kicked.**

My message to you is that you are not alone. Everyone has a peak, and everyone has a valley. My sense of you reading this book today is that you are either at the greatest peak or the deepest valley of your life, and no matter which place you are in, there are people here for you. We are creating the tribes of people who are here for

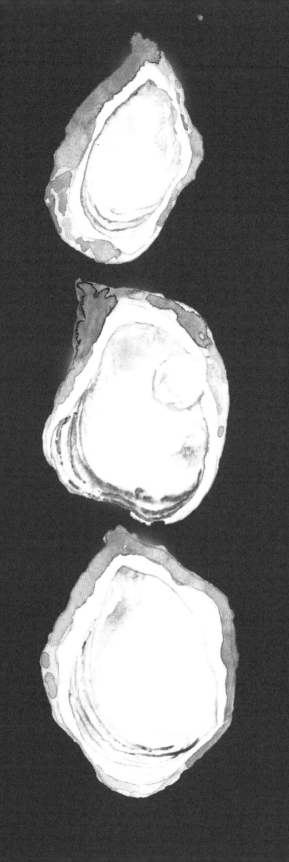

"It is not the critic who counts: not the man who points out how the strong man stumbles or where the doer of deeds could have done better. The credit belongs to the man who is actually in the arena, whose face is marred by dust and sweat and blood, who strives valiantly, who errs and comes up short again and again, because there is no effort without error or shortcoming, but who knows the great enthusiasms, the great devotions, who spends himself in a worthy cause; who, at the best, knows, in the end, the triumph of high achievement, and who, at the worst, if he fails, at least he fails while daring greatly, so that his place shall never be with those cold and timid souls who knew neither victory nor defeat."

—Theodore Roosevelt

each other, at the peak and at the valley, and the journey in between. That is what the *Empowerment Journey* is. Come along with us. Let's journey through the game of life. Because the game of life has paths that are always evolving from garden to mountain, valleys, peaks and canyons, to the shores that lead to oceans. We could use every path less traveled and still end up where we were meant to be. The path of joy, love, hope, suffering, awakening, enlightenment. For every blissful and amazing moment is the opposite, and we as humans are both. We are our greatest and glorious days, and we are our gloomiest and dark days. The bright side though, is that Source is with us always, from the beginning to end. God is Alpha and Omega, the Great I Am.

It doesn't matter if you believe in a God, Buddha, Gandhi, the astrological signs, or any other form of a higher and powerful being. So long as you believe in *something*, you will always have a guiding light, a lighthouse that will be your constant companion that glows within and around you. Learning to trust that what grows or flows into our lives will strengthen our souls. It will help us to become the beings we were meant to be here on this Earth.

People often forget that our lives become miserable when we forget the foundations of who we are. The danger starts when we focus entirely on things we cannot change, rather than what we can change. When we focus on what is out of our control, it can lead to frustration and bitterness. By understanding your own desires and motivations, you can change things far more than you realize.

I believe that our perfect life is waiting for us to let the lighthouse guide us back in from our sea of sorrow, pain, loss, and everything holding us back from living and loving our best selves and our best lives. The hope is that you and I get to have each other on this journey to empowerment. There is light at the end of this path.

We've just got to have the courage to go all in with Source and our purpose.

As we take a look back on where we've been and where we are going, we can see a trail of lifelong memories imprinting every version of ourselves in that specific moment of time. Using the tools we have, our compasses, maps, and guiding source of light, we can and we will overcome the trials we face.

The journey to becoming the best version of yourself is never easy. It all starts with deep reflection into your past—finding those defining moments that made you who you are today. Thinking about the traits that you have, good and bad, and why they are planted in the beginning of where you come from. Whether it's genetics or learned, the roots of *us* are *who we are* and the foundation of our existences. People are harming themselves because they forget who they are and the magic that they hold within themselves.

You are enough. You always have been, and you always will be. Take the time to get to know yourself again. From here on out, believe that you have a purpose here on this planet. You have roots to a lighthouse—everything in between will lead you to who you are meant to be.

Now that you've completed the book, I invite you to reevaluate your answers from before.

Who am I?

Who do I want to become in this life?

If I were to look up my name in the dictionary, what would it say?

If there were no limits, who would I be?

How would I define myself?

What do I want in all my dimensions of life?

Take a look at your dream board. What has changed? What remains? If you find parts of your written answers over the course of this book have offered you insight to a refined version of *you*, simply become that refined version you described. Adjust your board, and begin creating a new routine for yourself to accomplish the things you've set your heart and mind on. Trust your lighthouse in times of darkness and complete the journey of your soul.

Lesson Twenty

Dream Board Reflection

Purpose: Now that you've completed the book, I invite you to reevaluate what you thought was important and readjust anything that needs to be torn, shredded, or placed to the outer edges. This is the time to really hone in on your purpose and passions.

This lesson is a reflection of everything you have wanted to create from chapter 1 to the finish. Now it is update time. Revise your board to the newest dreams and wants for your life.

Tools:

- Vision board

- New pictures

- Goals

- Dreams

Activity: Who am I? Who do I want to become in this life? If I were to look up my name in the dictionary, what would it say? If there were no limits, who would I be? How would I define myself? What do I want in all my dimensions of life?

(20)

To Us

Dear Reader,

My soul's journey started in the cold of winter, fitting for my birth sign of Capricorn. I have taken you with me on a personal journey from the first seed of love planted by my parents that created the embryo Kimmy, to the hellebore weed that forever changed my trajectory. We left the garden of my youth to journey up the steep mountain path of discovery, acquisition, and knowledge. Each new climb brought triumphs, tears, and tragedies. With each new summit came opportunities to test my skills and talents I had developed from earlier climbs. It also exposed the buried boulders of rejection, betrayal, abandonment, shame, and fear. I learned to win, to lose, and to survive. The greatest losses came at the fate of lost loves and the death of loved ones. Those loves took with them a part of me. My anchors, partners, children—all left holes in the soul that only God's grace can heal.

After overcoming the big climbs and breathing the exhalation of success—basking in the glory of love, money, and accomplishments—the winds came, and the hurricane blew me off the summit out into the raging sea. There was crashing and thrashing and flailing and agony of defeat. I grabbed for the buoy for moments of rest and reprieve. There were glimmers of hope; moments that allowed my eyes to see the lighthouse calling me to the shore.

God promises that we will never be tested more than we can handle. Today, as I watched the first snowflakes from Heaven drop from the cold winter skies, I felt the chill of this long journey. I saw an angel in each flake, a promise of perfection, joy, and hope.

To my lost love, thank you for setting us free. For loving me enough to end our suffering. We resolved those unspoken agreements we made silently that held us both in our lack, limit, and untapped potential. I see the past in my rearview mirror of

words spoken; words I clung to like, "It's not our last time; we will be back." I feel the distance, the loss, the brutal pain of severed ties. The reality is there is no going back, and all of you have gone. Many doors have closed, and so many more have opened. Synchronistic miracles have happened perfectly since you drove away that cold winter day. God's hand has delivered me perfectly, showing me that around each bend was an angel to guide me on my path of passion and purpose.

A new love and a new career that serves others with my gift of teaching and story-telling. A love that is honest, kind, and unashamed. A love that desires to create a spiritual life of service to all souls on the journey. I know the miracles of God and how devastation led to creation, inspiration created thoughts, and my thoughts have created my path to purpose and passion.

My hope for each reader who picks up this book or hears my voice is that they will be inspired and empowered to implement the lessons I guide us through daily to get our lives on the path forward to passion and purpose. My wish is that my story will create believers in the infinite possibility of courage over comfort, determination over quitting, and the belief that thoughts become things. Never believe that you are not enough. Believe and do not lose faith. I know it is so hard sometimes to believe when hurting so badly. Trust me when I say, I have cried an ocean of tears; my soul has ached so badly I thought I was dying. It is imperative to remember, you are the author of your life's story. You hold the pen, and you write the ending. Choose amazing. God always sends that little buoy of red light flashing on the sea out in front of us, giving us one more ounce of hope and energy to keep swimming, floating, and breathing. I am so blessed by God's angels that reach down just as I think I cannot swim another stroke and carry me long enough to catch my breath, find inner peace, and go again.

I will never be able to explain the gratitude and love I have in my soul for all my divine guides, angels, and humans that consistently show up just in time. We are all part of the divine spirit, but our human experience will always involve trials, tribulations, glorious blessings, and huge amounts of success. I pray this teaching memoir of my life is an example to all my students in how to love, forgive, rejoice, and fight to live their best life...

The life that is always perfect, whole, and complete.

I love you,
Kimmy

Additional
Reading Materials

Daring Greatly by Dr. Brené Brown

The Four Agreements by Don Miguel Ruiz

The Gifts of Imperfection by Brené Brown

The Law of Attraction by Esther and Jerry Hicks

The Mastery of Love by Don Miguel Ruiz

A New Earth by Eckhart Tolle

The Power on Inspiration by Wayne Dyer

The Power of TED by David Emerald

The Power of Vulnerability by Brené Brown

Tears to Triumph by Marianne Williamson

About the Author

Kimberly (Kim or Kimmy) Anne Norman is a born teacher, author, entrepreneur, coach, traveler, and cook. She has lived a life of tears, tragedy, and triumph—from creating championship teams and successful companies that win, to pushing the envelope too far and experiencing heartbreaking failure.

The list goes on, but the trials and blessings have molded Kimmy into a firm believer that all souls can and do survive hard things. They learn that creating a humble gratitude for the tender mercies of life is essential. Her love for the art of communication sparks her passion to help others find their sole purpose in life: to be honest, vulnerable, and willing to connect while always seeking the Source of pure love and forgiveness.

Born in Moab, Utah, Kimmy was raised by parents who taught her the value of service to others and the ability to dream larger than the Universe. Her father, an exploration geologist, and mother, a Girl Scout leader and community advocate, enlightened her childhood through the principles of hard work, generosity, responsibility, and kindness to all in the community. She seeks to pass on this same wisdom to her readers through the stories, lessons, and recipes weaved throughout this book.

With over thirty years of experience coaching volleyball at the highest levels of the game, Kimmy has taught her teams that if they were not bonded, they would not battle. As a coach, educator, and entrepreneur, she brought the lesson of connection on and off the court, establishing three nonprofit organizations designed to serve women's empowerment through sports, leadership, and solid business principals. Kimmy continues to mentor people to believe in themselves, each other, and that anything is possible. She has coached Olympic athletes, mothers, doctors, attorneys, a Miss America runner up, and so many others. Each of them is a woman of power who is serving and leading with the same leadership values.

After completing her life-coaching certification, Kimmy began speaking and teaching on personal journeys, blending her career in education, sports, and our human spirit into the Empowerment Journey. Today, Kimmy is an international speaker and executive coach, guiding high achievers in connecting with their own Source and light to live and lead in their truth. The cornerstone of her life-coaching philosophy is her 5 Pillar (SOULS) system, which teaches people how to live their best lives through five steps: Success, Opportunities, Unleash, Leadership, Success.

Through the words written within these pages, Kimmy wishes to guide her readers to find the balance within your body, heart, mind, life, and soul. A believer in God and the Universal Power of Being, she invites us all to live by the parable of, "Be the change you want to see in the world."

Watch Kimmy speak at kimnormanspeaks.com
and learn more about her at empowermentjourney.com.